"Forgiving from the heart is
Pain of Offense. Only throu
and bless. This book helps
death and resurrection to release the provision for healthy and joyful
living."
John Sandford,   Founder, Elijah House

"The author of Escaping the Pain of Offense is a former student of
mine with an insightful and heart-felt approach to this important topic.
Seldom does a book on forgiveness weave theology, science, and
pastoral aspects of forgiveness into a form that is practically helpful.
Dr. Hersh does this beautifully. His emphasis on uncovering core
beliefs that hold hearts captive to the pain of unforgiveness can lead
you to deeper levels of intimacy with the Lord. His book is well-worth
your time and effort."
Fernando Garzon, Psy.D.,   Associate Professor, Liberty University

"Dr. Hersh captures the essence of forgiveness in a way that takes the
reader of Escaping the Pain of Offense to the heart of the matter. His
thorough study of the topic gives the reader wise counsel and practical
steps to follow towards wholeness."
E. Daniel Martin, MD,   Psychiatrist

"Finding freedom from emotional pain buried by long forgotten hurts
sometimes involves examining the source to allow God to show
you where the 'stuck point' occurred. Escaping the Pain of Offense
provides sharp insight to cut to the heart of the matter. It sensitively
leads you to Jesus as the true Healer of all life's hurts."
Frank   Meadows   LCSW,   Clinical   Director,   Christian
Psychotherapy Services and Founder of the Meadows Healing Prayer
Center in Chesapeake, Virginia

"Ed Hersh has astutely captured the essence of forgiveness in his
book Escaping the Pain of Offense. Ed's educational background,
discernment, and sensitivity to the Holy Spirit make him a qualified
person to address this topic with integrity and reliability."
Barry Wissler, Sr. Pastor,   Ephrata Community Church

"As a recent student of mine, Ed Hersh demonstrated knowledge
and commitment to the topic that makes this book well worth your
effort to explore. Escaping the Pain of Offense outlines key aspects
of forgiveness with biblical truth and action steps to greatly enhance
your walk with God."
Dr. Howard Dial,   Senior Pastor, Berachah Bible Church, Jonesboro,
Georgia

"The ministry of reconciliation is for all Christians, in all places, and spanning all times. The book Escaping the Pain of Offense helps Christ followers resolve conflict and pursue relationships reconciled through hearts surrendered to Jesus. This produces fruit to make the great commission a reality."
Dr. Roland Werner, General Secretary of CVIM (YMCA in Germany) and Founder of Christus-Treff Church in Germany (Marburg and Berlin) and Jerusalem

"Taking the bait of offense gives the enemy of God's people the greatest opportunity to pierce our prayer shield. Learn how Escaping the Pain of Offense can ward off the tormenters of our souls, invite God's presence into our midst, and make our prayers more effective. This is a vital topic to help you and your group experience health and well being."
Abby Abildness, President, Hershey Aglow; Healing Tree International

"Escaping the Pain of Offense will truly empower you to forgive from the heart. This book contains truth for healing of all peoples from varied cultures and backgrounds. Practicing forgiveness and reconciliation is key to unifying the Body of Christ."
Manny Roman, Pastor of Puerto de Refugio, a church in Lancaster, Pennsylvania

"There is little doubt that the topic of this excellent resource compiled by Edward Hersh will be relevant and helpful for all who have personally experienced struggles with forgiveness and reconciliation or are aware of others with a need to face those issues. I have known Ed to be passionately and compassionately focused in addressing these topics. He has combined a wealth of life experience with intense research to produce Escaping the Pain of Offense. As both a long-time friend of Ed's and one who has worked beside him in a variety of cultures, I know that this book will be a valuable tool and a useful addition to any library."
Evelyn Biles, President of Global Mosaic International

"Forgiveness, everyone talks about it, but few actually practice true forgiveness. Here's a book that will empower you to forgive from the heart. Challenging, engaging, and equipping for Escaping the Pain of Offense, your relationships with God and others will be deeply enriched."
Kenneth Martin, Senior Pastor, First Assembly of God, Hermitage, Pennsylvania

Escaping the Pain of Offense

ISBN 978-0-9893057-0-9

This title is also available in e-book format.

Find out more about the Blue Rock BnB Healing Ministry at: http://healing.bluerockbnb.com
Contact Ed at; 72 Blue Rock Road, Millersville, PA 17551
Ph: 717-872-7440
Email: hosts@bluerockbnb.com

Author's blog: http://authoredhersh.blogspot.com.

ESCAPING THE PAIN OF OFFENSE

Empowered to Forgive from the Heart

DR. EDWARD HERSH

Psalm 32

Blessings!,

EA

CONTENTS

DEDICATION

To my parents, wife, and children, those called
to be most forgiving of my shortcomings personally;

and to all who have been offended (victimized)
by an offender in the deepest sort of way;

and to the offenders owing the greatest debt,
whom God has called the offended to forgive,
for intentionally or unintentionally running up their debt.

And to God, the most gracious
Giver of the Gift of Forgiveness,
to Whom ALL praise and glory and honor
are due HIS Holy Name!

Acknowledgments

I would especially like to acknowledge by wife, Stephanie, who encouraged me the most through this project. Thanks also to all who helped by praying, editing, making suggestions, and participating in all the finer details of completing such a project.

Foreword

William Penn, founder of Pennsylvania and Delaware, wrote these words as he pondered the great possibilities of creating a "fresh start" in the Americas:

"There may yet be room for such a Holy Experiment. For the Nations want a precedent and my God will make it a Seed of a Nation, that an example may be set up to the Nations. That we may do the thing that is wise and just."

His "Holy Experiment" would establish a place where people could worship God and honor Christ without fear of persecution. Penn invited Anabaptists, Quakers and other persecution-weary peoples to live in the Americas, offering them a promise of religious freedom and a new beginning. This holy seed of *freedom* to worship God together was to serve as an example of true justice and wisdom to all the nations. His vision was to create a government of the people that reflected the Kingdom of God whose foundations are justice and righteousness. Isaiah 9 was a favored passage of his, especially that portion stating that the "government shall be upon His shoulders."

The Kingdom of God was to be reflected in the society of Pennsylvania. In Luke 9 and 10, this is revealed to be peace, healing, deliverance and new life. In addition to religious and political liberty Philadelphia was also the site of the first institutions of healing in the New World. The first hospital, medical school, pharmacy school, mental hospital, nursing school, osteopathic institute and other medical centers were developed in southeast Pennsylvania as the first of their kind in the United States. Therefore, it could also be expected that healing ministry and practical new models of Christian medical care should be a fruit of the historical blessing of our region. This pioneering of medical services in Philadelphia suggests that physical and emotional healing were also to be a "first fruit" of William Penn's Kingdom vision.

Penn also pioneered a new model for criminal justice. The development of the first penitentiary in the world occurred in Philadelphia. Instead of harsh corporal punishment common in England and the rest of the world in that time period, he created an institution with an atmosphere and structure that encouraged repentance, transformation and redemption of those incarcerated.

In the generation that followed his experiment, including the leadership provided by his own sons, these principles upon which he founded the Commonwealth were eroded. Greed for land and prosperity, among other factors, led to broken covenants and bloodshed in the region. Today much of what Penn dreamed has been buried and replaced. However, "our God is able to make all grace abound to" us (1 Cor. 9:8) such that we can believe for the restoring of many of the principles upon which this "Keystone" state was formed. It is time to believe again that we shall become "an example to the nations, a holy experiment." Let us re-dig our father's wells as Isaac did. As the people of God in this region, let us seize an opportunity to do "that which is wise and just"; to bring a restorative justice model to the state prison system.

All journeys begin the same—that is, with the first step. In 2002, a team of professionals and paraprofessionals working together initiated a Faith Enhanced Support (FES) program in the Lancaster County Prison (LCP). The FES program addressed mental health and addiction problems from a spiritual perspective in addition to the traditional medical treatment. Although the FES program ended at LCP in 2007, the numbers support a dramatic success for the initiative. Data gathered over the years during the FES program operation reveals a remarkable decrease in the amount of psychotropic medication prescriptions, mental health related commitments to hospitals and the overall cost of mental health services. The inmates' lives were impacted through development of meaningful relationships and successful endeavors upon their release from prison. The Faith-Enhanced Support program at the LCP made a significant difference in the community.

In 2008, a similar model of care called the Refuge of Healing and Hope (RHH) was initiated at the Water Street Medical Clinic in Lancaster, PA. RHH is a project of Light of Hope CSO, and is a collaboration of individuals, churches, and ministries who work together to provide treatment to the whole person including spiritual, emotional and physical needs based in the belief that true healing comes through Jesus Christ. RHH seeks to integrate professional and paraprofessional services to form a team approach to treating medical and mental health needs with spiritual care and faith-based services.

Medical conditions are often related to a person's spiritual health. Research has shown that physical problems are commonly rooted in emotional and mental health concerns. Examining how the spirit, mind, body, and soul function together to make a whole person, can significantly enhance a patient's recovery and overall health. In addition to the traditional treatment medical science provides, helping participants discover and remove the blockages keeping them from experiencing God as their *healer*, is the mission of the Refuge of Healing and Hope.

Ed Hersh carries this vision and mission close to his heart. He has been an integral part of the work of Refuge of Healing and Hope, helping us expand our efforts from the prison setting to a medical clinic and family medical practice in the community near Lancaster. In authoring *Escaping the Pain of Offense: Empowered to Forgive from the Heart*, he outlines key principles for being set free from spiritual bondage. He addresses vital areas of heart transformation and reveals necessary elements in conflict resolution and reconciliation in relationships.

In addition to the fruit of many lives positively touched by the healing power of God, the efforts of RHH and groups with like-minded vision, are transforming the spiritual atmosphere of our region. As we join together as medical professionals, business leaders, a criminal justice system, government leaders, churches and human service communities, we believe to see a renewing of the hope and dream of our founding fathers. We invite you to join with us in this journey of "back to the future." As we look back we may actually move the "Seed of the Nation" from hibernation to life. Hebrews 11:39-40 summarizes this thought; "And all these (ancestors), having obtained a good testimony through faith, did not receive the promise, God having provided something better for us, that they should not be made perfect apart from us."

Robert Doe, MD
Executive Director, Light of Hope Community Service
Organization

PREFACE

Very often I share the principle with people that "in order to be change agents, we must be changed agents." We have nothing to give in life (and ministry) except that which we have received from the Lord. Nowhere is this truer than with the topic at hand. Understanding unforgiveness and forgiveness more deeply and becoming a better forgiver comes with an extremely high price. Becoming more knowledgeable about forgiveness incurs a stricter judgment, as James 3:1 explains. However, experiencing the rewards of deeper levels of God's grace makes it worth it all.

I recently completed a Doctor of Religious Studies (DRS) degree at Trinity Theological Seminary. A murder took place in our community on November 13, 2005 which greatly influenced my decision to choose this topic as the research project for the DRS degree. An eighteen year old Christian youth who was scheduled to graduate with home schoolers in our daughter's class the next spring, killed Michael and Kathy Borden, friends of ours through home school and church activities. The Bordens' fourteen year old daughter was being pursued by the young man. On that Sunday morning after a discussion in the Borden's home that didn't go his way; he pulled a gun and shot them in their home in Lititz, PA.

Ten months later another murderous tragedy occurred in our community when Carl Roberts killed five young girls, wounded five others, and killed himself in an Amish school house. Our family has lots of friends and church acquaintances familiar with the killer in this incident as well. As shocking and puzzling as these events are, equally troubling is the seeming unwillingness on the part of many in the Christian Church to ask the hard questions in an effort to determine and deal with the root issues which led to the tragedies. What conditions in the Church allowed a professing Christian to harbor evil in his heart to the degree of taking such aggressive actions and becoming a murderous predator of the innocent? At times like these, life often presents us with many more questions than answers. However, not having answers or even being afraid of the possible answers, should not keep us from asking the questions.

Neither of the two cases mentioned above involved a history of psychiatric illness on the part of the perpetrator. Many times, however, a mental health diagnosis adds to the complexity of the Christian's ability to arrive at the heart of a problem. Labeling an addiction as an illness, for example, sometimes complicates the treatment and diminishes the chances for breaking free in the spirit of a person. A person's physical health and emotional condition are often connected to his or her spiritual condition. Relationship problems inevitably stem from sinful roots of unforgiveness. The writer of Hebrews exhorts, "See to it that no one falls short of the grace of God and that no bitter root grows up to cause trouble and defile many" (Heb. 12:15).

Primary attention, therefore, must be given to a person's spiritual health. One may ask how another book on forgiveness could add anything unique to the literature already produced on the topic. While many great books exist, as I explain in the introduction, much confusion still exists among Christians about forgiveness. It is my hope that the personal experiences and insights gained in counseling and working with many other human beings, like myself, will help to stimulate a hunger in the reader to reengage the immeasurably bottomless topic of forgiveness. This book addresses a Christian view of forgiveness. May it help the reader apply the truth needed in order to escape the bondage and imprisonment of the bitterness, resentment and blame that is caused by offense.

Part One—Foundations

Chapter One

Introduction: The Cycle of Offense

The Old Testament prophet Isaiah uses the imagery of imprisonment to communicate the condition of mankind and the mission of Jesus Christ to set us free.

> The Spirit of the Sovereign LORD is on me,
> because the LORD has anointed me
> to proclaim good news to the poor.
> He has sent me to bind up the brokenhearted,
> to proclaim freedom for the captives
> and release from darkness for the prisoners,
> to proclaim the year of the LORD's favor
> and the day of vengeance of our God,
> to comfort all who mourn,
> and provide for those who grieve in Zion—
> to bestow on them a crown of beauty
> instead of ashes,
> the oil of joy
> instead of mourning,
> and a garment of praise

instead of a spirit of despair.
They will be called oaks of righteousness,
a planting of the LORD
for the display of his splendor. (Isa. 61:1-3)

As explained later, the poor, brokenhearted captive describes every person who ever lived including all of us today. Jesus came to *proclaim liberty* to that condition for all who believe in Him. In Matthew 18 Jesus himself uses an illustration of a debtor's prison to show the condition of the human heart and the need for salvation from being "handed over to the jailers to be tortured" (Matt. 18:34). Torment "is how my heavenly Father will treat each of you unless you forgive your brother or sister from your heart" (Matt. 18:35). Again, these verses will be discussed more later, but for now let us understand that the Bible clearly connects a lack of forgiveness with imprisonment, hurt and pain in the human heart.

How is this hurt produced? We are hurt through taking offense. How does the offense imprison our heart? Our heart is imprisoned by building fences: walls of perceived security. These walls not only trap the pain inside, but they often keep out troops sent to rescue the prisoner. When we take the bait of the Enemy's offense, we become offended and imprisoned in a cycle shown in the illustration.

The Cycle of Offense

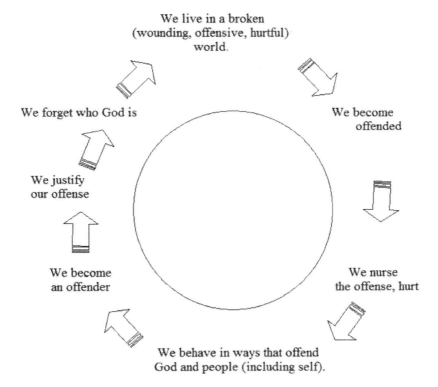

We live in a broken
(wounding, offensive, hurtful)
world.

We forget who God is

We become
offended

We justify
our offense

We become
an offender

We nurse
the offense, hurt

We behave in ways that offend
God and people (including self).

This cycle is common to each of us. Because we live in a fallen, broken, and imperfect world, experiencing hurtful emotions is inevitable.

We become wounded by peoples' mistakes, misunderstandings, mistreatments, betrayals, injustices, abuses or even crimes.

We nurse the wound by rehearsing in our minds what coulda', woulda', shoulda' been done to avoid the pain. Many times our anger becomes directed at God for allowing bad things to happen to us. Some blame self, and become imprisoned by self-rejection.

We make ungodly judgments and behave in ways that offend God, us, and other people. Thus, *we become an offender*. Bitterness, resentment and blame become an accepted way of life. Without God's help we try to rectify situations in many ways including revenge, obsessing for justice, forgetting, excusing, "moving on," self-inflicting condemnation, or finding some other way of replacing the negative feelings with positive ones.

In our quest of human effort we may even find some relief, and so *we justify our offense.* Unable to surrender to (trust) God the sole right to judge our offender, we reject God's provision through Jesus to break the cycle. Having agreed with the lie that holding offense solves our problem, we become offensive to someone else who becomes offended, and the cycle spirals hopelessly on.

There is hope! Our hope is in Jesus and what God has done through Him.[1] Through God's Gift of forgiveness, we not only have hope to redeem this cycle in our own lives, but we can reverse this spiral in the lives of others as well. You do not have to be enslaved by this victim/predator cycle. Stress, anxiety, and depression no longer have to remain when you allow Christ Jesus into the deepest parts of your heart to break this cycle down.

The Cross and Resurrection of Jesus is the only true jailbreak for unforgiveness. Therefore, a significant portion of this book will discuss the fundamentals of God's purpose and plan through salvation in Jesus Christ. Before that, in Part One, we must discuss some background and rationale for a Christian handling of the topic of forgiveness.

In Part Two we will discuss the human response to Christ's accomplishments. The greatest hindrance to breaking free seems to be recognizing the imprisonment. Sometimes we have become so well-adjusted to imprisonment, it seems hard to imagine what true freedom is really like. Some of us like the comforts in prison. Some of us like the security it provides. Some like the decisions made for them and some are apathetic about change. Some doubt their ability to succeed at a better way, and many are just simply in denial about their condition or unwilling to change their perceptions. We all choose living in illusion over reality to some degree. Breaking free occurs from the inside out. As you walk out of the inner most cell, you come to the next barred gate. As you break free of the next courtyard and the next and so on, you eventually come to the outer court and can maneuver to leap the outer fence. This is when you realize that the offense that took you to prison (whether self-inflicted or inflicted by another offender) no longer has a grip on your life.

In Part Three we discuss how this new freedom in the inner man can change your relationships with other people. God made mankind for community. Relationship with other people can only be experienced in the deepest way God meant for them to be shared when each individual has broken free of his own prison experience. Each person's receiving God's love and giving that love to others is our mission as we journey in the freedom of forgiveness.

Appendix A contains some additional resources for the reader's equipping and edification.

Appendix B shares a small portion of the author's personal story and how practicing forgiveness has transformed his life.

Appendix C is the contents of a pamphlet written by the author and his wife many years ago. The pamphlet was widely distributed across the U.S. and around the globe in an effort to help women (and men) struggling with abortion.

The Endnotes at the end the book for Parts One, Two, and Three contain references to Bible portions and books and articles further cited in the Bibliography at the end of this book.

How to Use this Book

- Read the three chapters in Part One and then read and process the Follow up and Practice material for Part One.
- Then read the chapters in Part Two and do the Follow up and Practice for Part Two.
- And then Part Three in the same manner.
- Return to the book weeks or months later to re-process the Follow up and Practice material or process the remaining material not finished in the initial reading.
- A Study Guide is provided at the end of the book to be used as a ten session small group or individual study.

The journey to healing is often like peeling an onion: to arrive at the core, the outer visible layers must be taken off first. The Follow up and Practice material provides some exercises for processing the material in each part for deeper understanding and application. You will understand why this is as you read. My suggestion is that you adopt a "long haul" and "forever growing" perspective of allowing God to change your heart. As you do, you will increasingly see fruit in your relationship with God and with others around you. As you grow, asking yourself the same questions as before may elicit different answers, reflecting your expanding and deepening perceptions, healing, and maturity.

Our understanding and practice of forgiveness holds the key to freedom. Before we consider what releases freedom, let us look at some of the obstacles and misunderstandings.

CHAPTER TWO

FORGIVENESS: MISUNDERSTANDINGS

Although a familiar topic to Christians, for many the true meaning of forgiveness evades their understanding and practice. The mystery of forgiveness contains inexhaustible elements for study, in which we apply ever greater depths of wisdom and knowledge. Forgiveness becomes less of a mystery when the Creator's purpose and plan are understood and accepted by the creation. Below are a few justifications which warrant a clearer biblical understanding of forgiveness and greater devotion to its practice in today's world.

Relational Conflict Indicators Among Christians

Christian apologetics author Josh McDowell has researched Christian youths' behaviors for years. An alarming trend is the lack of convictions and belief in absolute truth.[1] Eroding beliefs on standards of morality and Christian faith undeniably impact relationships in a negative direction. The lack of value for human life as evidenced by increases in abortion, infanticide, and euthanasia are some indirect results of this erosion. Other more direct results involve moral declines, breakdown of the family unit, church and community conflicts, and crime at rapidly increasing rates. More Christians than ever are becoming entangled in the consequences of acting on a non-biblical worldview. As a Barna 2006 survey points out, although large majorities of the public claim to be "deeply spiritual" and say that their religious faith is "very important" in their lives, only 15 percent of those who regularly attend a Christian church ranked their relationship with God as the top priority in their lives.[2]

Mental Health Problems Increasing

With personal problems and relational conflict on the increase, more people are seeking mental health treatment. Increased mental and emotional difficulties can be attributed to higher stress levels and pressures of modern life. The use of psychotropic medications is on the increase and mental health diagnoses and addiction problems are more common than ever before. The pharmaceutical industry in general is stronger than ever and substance abuse seems rampant, not only in "high risk" populations, but also across the social and economic spectrum of society.

Psychotic disorders, some caused by biological conditions, are much rarer than less severe conditions, such as so-called adjustment and mood disorders. Even for non-psychotic diagnoses, however, medications are commonly used as a primary mode of treatment. Modes of treatment for depression and other common conditions seem to focus much more attention on symptoms as opposed to examining root issues of these problems. Modern psychotherapy seems to favor techniques of managing behaviors through cognitive exercises rather than transforming the character of an individual. Temporary relief may help, but removing the source of the problem is even better.

Lack of Forgiveness Is a Root Issue Often Overlooked

Holistic healing has become a more familiar topic in recent times. The body, mind, and spirit of a person are intrinsically connected, and sometimes etiological sources of sickness are not easily determined. Physical symptoms may be caused by emotional and/or spiritual conditions in the individual. Although God's plan of healing for a person may encompass the physical, psychological, and spiritual dimensions, sinful roots such as bitterness and resentment often are overlooked in terms of significance and impact on a person's overall health.[3] Barna's research indicates an added complication for Christians in that Christians' spirituality is having less of an impact on their world-view and lifestyle.[4]

Forgiveness Is Significantly Misunderstood

Although forgiveness is a familiar topic to Christians, a great deal of confusion exists concerning its practice and application to life experiences. Many consider it a virtue and even agree to the centrality of forgiveness in the gospel message, but few can articulate a biblical view of the transforming power of forgiveness. According to a Barna survey completed in August 1999, approximately four out of ten participants acknowledged they were struggling with forgiving someone.[5] If an accurate estimate, this percentage translates to fifty-five to sixty million people in the United States who are dealing with unforgiveness—bitterness, resentment, vengeful desires, and/or avoidance. As a subset of the total, roughly one in four (23 percent) born-again Christians, and one in ten (10 percent) evangelical Christians, reported being unable (not distinguished from unwilling) to forgive someone in their lives.[6]

Barna distinguished evangelical from born-again Christians through seven additional criteria—summarized in general by belief in orthodox doctrine, and in particular by the exclusivity of the gospel and the authority and inerrancy of the Bible.[7] Furthermore, the survey posed five myths associated with forgiveness and used them as the criteria for determining whether or not the respondents had a biblical worldview on forgiveness. The five myths are as follows: (1) "Forgiveness should be granted only if the offending individual shows remorse." (2) "True forgiveness requires that the offending party be released from the consequences of his or her actions." (3) "True forgiveness requires that the forgiver re-establish a relationship with the offending person." (4) "True forgiveness means that the forgiver must also forget what was done." (5) "There are some crimes, offenses, or other things that people do to one another that can never be forgiven."

Based on these criteria, the survey shows that only 4 percent of respondents disagreed with all five myths. Comparatively, only 5 percent of born-again Christians and only 8 percent of evangelical Christians disagreed with all five myths. However, respondents who strongly disagreed with three of the five myths were classified as possessing a biblical understanding of forgiveness. Of the total respondents, 20 percent were classified as biblical forgivers, while 25 percent of born-again Christians and 40 percent of evangelical Christians were placed in this category. The survey concludes that most people do not practice biblical forgiveness primarily because of a nonbiblical understanding of the subject.[8]

Compounding the problem of not understanding forgiveness is the equally damaging effects of not understanding unforgiveness. A right understanding of unforgiveness is imperative, since it will have a direct impact on the direction one takes to move towards forgiveness. The majority of discussion about unforgiveness does not extend beyond the issues of relief of emotional stress or hurtful cognitions. The concept of "sin" seems of little consequence even in many Christian circles. Focusing on humanity without concern for the divine keeps the unbelieving areas of the heart hidden from the truth.

The writer of Hebrews clearly warns against allowing sin to fester in the heart. "See to it, brothers, that none of you has a sinful, unbelieving heart that turns away from the living God." (Heb. 3:12) The entire book of Hebrews is devoted to the centrality of Christ as the basis of life experience. Furthermore, verses like the following are scattered through the entire New Testament: "But I am afraid that just as Eve was deceived by the serpent's cunning, your minds may somehow be led astray from your sincere and pure devotion to Christ" (2 Cor. 11:3). Cunningham sums up the dilemma of misunderstanding forgiveness and implicitly alludes to the sin associated with unforgiveness: "We know a lot more about the need for forgiveness than we know about the power to forgive. Perhaps that's because many of us know more about our kinship with Adam and Eve than we may know about our kinship with Christ."[9]

Recent Research

Throughout the last twenty years, forgiveness research has become an increasingly popular area of study within the fields of psychology and theology. Recently, psychological studies have focused on factors that influence individuals to forgive, the conditions under which one is more likely to forgive, and the implications these findings have for clinical settings. Within the past few years, in order to increase effectiveness of forgiveness interventions, scientific research has begun to explore what specific components within various interventions may be necessary to encourage forgiveness.

A number of models and different types of techniques have been used in forgiveness research. To date, the two intervention models that have been most commonly used are Worthington's Model known as REACH Forgiveness and the Enright Forgiveness Model. Although researchers seem to agree that therapeutic interventions are helpful, not all agree on the efficacy of forgiveness interventions. Not surprisingly, major researchers in the field note that there is a divergence among researchers in the definitions of forgiveness.[10] Although not always explicitly addressed, there are many variations associated with the conceptual understanding of forgiveness. Some of these involve reasons and consequences of unforgiveness, motives for forgiveness, the issue of conditionality, the actual process of forgiveness, the relationship between forgiveness and reconciliation, and even the timing and types of forgiveness.

Two foundational reasons drive the divergent understandings and their assorted emphases within the field of forgiveness research. The first involves a clash of world-views between modern psychology and Christian theology. Modern psychology is based on naturalistic and humanistic world-views centered on the experiences of men and women, whereas an orthodox Christian theology is centered on God and is based on the authority of Scripture. Secondly, to remain consistent with the method of modern science, empirical research is generally segregated from issues of faith and theology. Therefore, the forgiveness of God and one's dynamic, personal relationship with Him are typically absent from the vast majority of empirical research conducted in the last two decades.[11]

To summarize, the depth and richness of biblical instruction on forgiveness has not been related to contemporary research on forgiveness and the practice of clinical counseling. Consequently, the clinical concept of interpersonal forgiveness was explicitly developed solely with reference to human-to-human relationships with little to no regard for its divine context. Since practical application is inextricably linked to one's theoretical understanding, one's concept and given definition of forgiveness determine how forgiveness is or is not carried out. A Christian definition of forgiveness must originate not from humanity's perspective, but from God's perspective.

My own doctoral research study led me to the following thesis.

> In order for a forgiveness intervention to be most successful in a Christian's mental health treatment and spiritual growth, understanding and applying a God-centered approach which emphasizes the finished work of Christ and progressive sanctification affords the most fruitful results.[12]

For the Christian, forgiveness does not chiefly depend on the ability to empathize or relate to the offender in some manner. An understanding of forgiveness must be lived out through a personal relationship with Jesus Christ. Christ has accomplished forgiveness through his death and resurrection, and the power of one human to forgive another comes through transformation of the inner person. Applying forgiveness with the theological understanding of progressive sanctification becomes a primary intervention, and preferable to a purely therapeutic intervention. As a divine work, the supernatural intervenes to make a way for the natural broken response of the human heart.

The next chapter is the most important in the book. Read it in its entirety. Do not allow yourself to be tempted to skip any portion of it to "move on" to more exciting topics. As God's beloved creation, it doesn't get any more adventurous and challenging than to be rescued from the debtor's prison we find ourselves in.

CHAPTER THREE

FORGIVENESS: DIVINELY INITIATED

Two focus statements serve as the target for this chapter. First, the Christian understanding of forgiveness must be contextualized in purposes of God's redemptive history. Second, biblical understanding of forgiveness must be centered on the foundational framework of the life, death, and resurrection of Jesus Christ.

In the Introduction we considered how this topic is important in the scheme of present-day cultural relevance. The material in this chapter focuses on the relevance of a God in a larger picture of truth and historical context. The topic of forgiveness cannot be separated from the Author of forgiveness and indeed the Creator of all things. Without God in the picture, more questions arise about forgiveness than will ever be answered.

Redemptive History

Many struggling individuals often deal with their problems in isolation. Not only do they withdraw from others, but the larger problem is their withdrawal from God. Man's rebellion against God has existed since the first sins of Adam and Eve.[1] A myopic view of life allows the struggles and difficulties to take center stage. Little hope and much despair on the periphery makes getting beyond the brokenness and the pain seem impossible.

Much of the brokenness is often rooted in a heart condition known as unforgiveness (i.e. ungodly judgments, bitterness, resentment and the like). The temporal struggles are indeed real, but the reality is that one's tragic story is actually a subplot within a larger drama that transcends the shame, despair, and pain associated with the individual human struggle. Therefore, one's individual ordeal must be viewed through the lens of God's panoramic story of redemption.[2]

From Genesis to Revelation, Scripture makes known God's sovereign, redemptive work in the history of humanity. The Old and the New Testaments both point to Jesus Christ as the central figure in this salvation drama.[3] In Christ, God stepped from eternity and entered time and space through the incarnation of the Son of God. The life, death, and resurrection of Christ had divine purposes—to bring glory to God by demonstrating justice and mercy through grace and love. Christ taught the essence of forgiveness and love through his teaching and death.[4]

Therefore, a Christ-centered understanding and definition of forgiveness must be rooted in God's redemptive history, sprouting from the rich ground of God's love and forgiveness, and bearing fruit that is consistent with the summation of God's Law of love, as taught by the One who called Himself the Truth. God's redemptive history consists of four phases; Creation, the Fall, Redemption, and Consummation.[5] All that God created was good; however, the need for forgiveness arose with the fall of humanity, or the emergence of sin against God and others. Redemption, which includes the forgiveness of sins, is found only in the work of Jesus Christ on the cross. At the end of history, with the advent of the new heaven and earth, forgiveness will no longer be needed when sin and death are abolished; however, those who will spend eternity with God in Christ will always be known as forgiven sinners, saved by grace.

The Unbroken World—Creation

From the opening chapters of Genesis, two main themes emerge as foundational principles. Every person is created in God's image and every person is created to be in relationship; first and foremost, in relationship with God, and second, in relationship with others. Not only were heaven and earth created, but community was created between God and His people, and between the first man and woman. God formed the man and woman in His own image[6] and breathed into them the breath of life, [7] doing so with much care and loving knowledge.[8] God created man and woman ultimately for His own glory.[9] Every person has extraordinary value and inherent worth, [10] since each person is made by God to bear His image and to worship Him. In the Garden of Eden, God also created a paradise of mutuality, consisting of trust and unity of fellowship with God and others. Perfect love flowed first and foremost within the Trinity, then within the garden during this first period of redemptive history. The need for forgiveness did not exist. The first humanity enjoyed intimacy not only with each other, but with the perfect community that exists within the triune God.

Being created in God's image has some implications with regards to forgiveness. The fact that finite human beings are made to reflect the image of their infinite Creator allows for at least three broad inferences. First, people are more than flesh and blood. Every person is an embodied soul, with a spirit that will live for an eternity. Although a fascinating topic, biblical anthropology cannot be elaborated in this book. Next, relationships between people are of value and affirm their worth in God's sight. Thus, an essential element of forgiveness is that every person has worth and is meant to live in a peaceful, unified relationship with others. Inherent to God's moral attributes—goodness, love, mercy, etc. (Grudem 1994)—is the aspect of relationality. Virtues such as love, kindness, and mercy exist only within the context of relationships. Therefore, it seems likely that these relational virtues are involved when dealing with forgiveness and relational offenses. Third, it can be reasoned that every person, being made by God as His representative, is meant to live according to His ways, as a reflection of his Creator. It makes sense that the One who created humanity knows what is best for His creation. Scripture gives abundant guidance for relationships—how to love, to forgive, and to create unity for the purpose of God-glorifying community.

The Broken World—Fall

The second scene of God's providential history is revealed when the first man and woman turned and rebelled against God[11] by submitting their wills to the evil will of Satan, a powerful being,[12] yet far inferior to God. This act of defiance brought about two deaths; the inevitable physical death and the more immediate and significant spiritual death that separated them from the presence of the holy God.

The sin of Adam and Eve resulted in the moral depravity[13] of every descendant after them. They also experienced shame and guilt[14] after realizing they were naked and had sinned against God. They no longer enjoyed the privileged and intimate relationship with their Creator. They no longer were perfect reflectors of God's image. Foolishly, they withdrew from the only One who could offer safe refuge and deliver them from this dilemma; however, they also withdrew because of God's fearsome holiness, knowing that they fully deserved His wrath. When questioned by God about their actions, the man defended himself by blaming both God and the woman,[15] and the woman, in turn, blamed her actions and attitude on the serpent.[16] Humanity's relationship with God was broken. The interpersonal relationship between the first man and woman was damaged, and the created order was disordered.

The entrance of sin resulting from man's rebellion against God provides a host of implications for forgiveness. First and foremost, the need for forgiveness was established after the dark stain of sin ruined the perfection of the Creation.

Second, because of the sinful heart of humanity,[17] relationships with God and others are hindered and damaged, resulting in deep pain and shame. Unfortunately, broken hearts are the norm in a fallen world; there will always be a need to forgive and be forgiven.

Third, rebellion against God's ways leads to a withdrawal from Him, the source of perfect love. Sin also breaks trust with God and causes one to question the goodness, faithfulness, and justice of God, and distorts the truth of who He is. Fourth, the deceit and distortion of sin hinders one's ability to overcome the feelings and actions associated with unforgiveness (hatred, bitterness, resentment, and vengeful emotions). It causes one to view the offender as a despicable, evil person. Finally, sin intensifies the focus upon oneself, and diminishes the vision of God and others. Self-righteousness, self-absorption, self-protection, self-service, and self-justice become the mantra in the meditation and rumination of unforgiveness.

The Redeemed World

Even before the creation of time, the eternal Father, by His pleasure and in the mystery of His good and perfect will, saw the *need* for forgiveness because of the sin to come. God intended for His Son to be the means through which He would redeem His people from the wages of sin, thus *revealing* the ultimate portrait of forgiveness and love in the cross of Christ. God, being rich in mercy and great in His love for His people,[18] offered the perfect solution to the problem of sin that soils and separates everyone from Him. God sent His Son Jesus Christ, who lived a sinless life, to be a perfect sacrifice for His people. A perfect sacrifice was required to satisfy a holy God.

God demonstrated His divine love by dying for His enemies, justifying them by His blood and saving them from His wrath.[19] By grace through faith in Jesus Christ[20] one is forgiven of sin and declared righteous before God, all because of the substitutionary and final work of His Son Jesus Christ on the cross.[21] "Whoever believes in him shall not perish."[22] God's merciful redemption is even foreshadowed in creation when God shed the blood of animals to cover the shameful nakedness of Adam and Eve before they were exiled from the Garden.[23]

Redemption involves relational restoration, and implications abound for forgiveness from this phase of redemptive history. First, through the work of divine forgiveness, the pathway was made to reconcile individuals with God, thus restoring personal intimacy with their Creator through justification in

Christ. Second, through the work of redemption, each of God's children is re-created with a new heart, spirit, and identity in Christ, along with a new perspective, a desire for God, and access to supernatural love and grace. In other words, through the forgiveness of sins, one who has been saved by grace can begin the process of being restored to a truer image of God through the journey of sanctification.[24] Third, God revealed divine forgiveness through the cross of Christ, thus providing the supreme and authoritative paradigm for His people to emulate; forgive "just as God in Christ also has forgiven you."[25] Finally, God revealed His great love through forgiveness for the sake of His glory and to make His power known.[26]

The Consummated World

Redemptive history can be described as God's love story, starting with God lovingly creating the heavens and earth, along with the divinely appointed marriage between the first man and woman, and ending with the ultimate, everlasting marriage— the wedding between Christ and His bride, the church.[27] From God's perspective, this marriage represents the supreme, most significant relationship that will ever exist, aside from the Trinity. God is forever wedded to His people in an intimacy that He has compared to marriage.[28] What are some of the other significant truths about the end of the age? The end of redemptive history is also associated with the final judgment of all humanity, the final and ultimate vengeance of God, the final and complete restoration of the image of God, and the final community of God's people.

At first glance, one might too easily dismiss the significance of the consummation in dealing with forgiveness. Aside from redemption, this last, but all important phase of God's history provides substantial implications for the topic at hand. First, love reigns supreme for all of eternity. Perfect love found within the Trinity will also exist within the marriage union between Christ and His bride in the consummated kingdom. Thus, the temporality of forgiveness should be understood within the context of the eternality of love. Next, the future reality of God's final judgment and vengeance is an undeniable truth which must be factored into a God-centered model of forgiveness. Faith in the One who is the righteous Judge is essential if one is to give up one's thoughts of self-justice or revenge in order to place them in the hands of the Lord. To act with malice and hatred towards the offender is not only displeasing to God, but discounts His future judgment and undermines His redemptive power in the life of those impacted and involved in any moral offense.[29]

Moreover, present solace must be found in the future grace of God's finished work in the body and soul of every believer. Promise of completed redemption gives the offended person hope in dealing with irreparable injuries and in forgiving the offender who seems to be unredeemable. This perspective demands a deep faith in the Redeemer and requires unselfish concern for the souls of others. For the one who seeks forgiveness, the truth of future glory encourages one to press on, under the gracious and forgiving love of God, despite the unforgiveness of the other.

Furthermore, developing a vision of fullness of joy and pleasures in the presence of the Lord, enjoyed within a community of brothers and sisters in Christ, causes one to crave such divine and pure unity. People can overcome much adversity with an overwhelming and powerful vision of hope and love. Finally, the need to forgive will no longer exist in the consummated era.

With salvation complete, all of God's children will stand forever righteous before the Father in Christ. With death swallowed up in victory and sin put to death, relationships will flourish in the environment of perfect love,[30] and forgiveness will no longer be needed. In other words, love will continue long after the need for forgiveness comes to an end.

Jesus the Savior

Nowhere is God's redemptive plan for humanity more visible than in the atonement. One's view of the atonement will shape everything else of what one believes about forgiveness.[31] Fallen humanity cannot truly understand God's forgiveness. Personal struggles with forgiving other people often lead to projecting one of two perspectives on God. Some people find it impossible to envision Almighty God as anything other than stern and unforgiving. Others, knowing that Scripture teaches us God is merciful, imagine that He is so completely indulgent that no sinner really has anything to fear. Both misconceptions are erroneous concerning divine forgiveness.[32]

Furthermore, although everyone recognizes justice and mercy as great virtues, responses to these virtues may differ depending on which side of the equation is warranted. When forgiveness is needed on the receiving end, mercy is esteemed. An aggrieved party, however, may see forgiveness as a violation of justice. How can these two virtues be reconciled, if not from a human point of view, from a divine perspective?

God is a God of perfect justice and perfect mercy. He cannot simply choose to declare all offenses null and void, excusing sin and letting the sinner go unpunished. God cannot and will not simply acquit transgressors by ignoring the evil they have done. God is a god of absolute righteousness and absolute grace. Both truths must be kept in balance if we are to understand what Scripture teaches about forgiveness.

Perfect Justice

The Bible repeatedly confirms that God will punish every sin. God's law of sowing and reaping, for example, gives us a clear warning: "Do not be deceived, God is not mocked; for whatever a man sows, this he will also reap" (Gal. 6:7). In Exodus 23:7 God says, "I will not acquit the guilty." Nahum 1:3 relates unequivocally, "The LORD will by no means leave the guilty unpunished." Declaring the gospel message itself, Paul says, "God's wrath is revealed . . . against all ungodliness and unrighteousness" (Rom. 1:18). The relationship between God and the sinner is described as enmity.[33] God hates sin, and therefore all who sin have made themselves God's enemies. "God is angry with the wicked every day" (Ps. 7:11 King James Version). He hates those who do iniquity.[34]

All people are born with an insatiable penchant for sin.[35] They are spiritually dead, reveling in their own sin, objects of God's holy anger and utterly without hope[36] All sinners are in the same boat. Those who violate some minor point of God's law are as guilty as if they had broken every commandment.[37] The real truth is that no one's sins are trivial.[38] From the human perspective, this is a truly desperate state of absolute futility.

God, on the other hand, is perfect, infinitely holy, absolutely flawless, and thoroughly righteous. His justice must be satisfied by the punishment of every violation of His law. And the due penalty of man's iniquity is infinitely severe: eternal damnation. Nothing fallen humanity can offer God could possibly atone for sin, because the price of sin is too high.

The situation seems irreversible for the human race: we are accountable to a holy God whose justice must be satisfied, and yet we are guilty sinners, incapable of doing anything whatsoever to satisfy God's justice. Left to ourselves, we would all be doomed. We are guilty by virtue of "being," having inherited the human genetic code.

Perfect Mercy

However, for those who believe in Jesus, [39] Scripture tells us that God *does* justify the ungodly. He covers their transgressions. He refuses to take their misdeeds into account. [40] He declares them righteous, completely forgiving their sins. The gospel is such great news!

How can God grant such forgiveness without compromising His own standard of justice? How can He justify sinners without rendering Himself unjust? How can He forgive sinners without breaking His own word, having already sworn that He will punish every transgression? The answer is this: God Himself has made His Son, Jesus Christ, the atonement for our sins.

As described in the previous chapter, a significant discrepancy exists between Christian belief and practice on the topic of forgiveness. What is needed to correct this discrepancy is a fresh grasp and new appreciation for the truth about Christ's substitutionary work as the most vital of all Christian doctrines. This truth lies at the very heart of the gospel message. It is the most glorious truth in all of Scripture. It explains how God can remain just while justifying sinners, [41] and it is the only hope for any sinner seeking forgiveness.

Christ Accomplishes Forgiveness

Jesus Christ came to earth to reconcile humanity unto God. This ministry of reconciliation is the heartbeat of Christianity and what distinguishes it from all other religions.[42] Perhaps the most important single passage in all of Scripture about Christ's substitution on sinners' behalf is found in the book of 2 Corinthians, chapter 5.[43] Notice how the idea of forgiveness permeates the context. In fact, *reconciliation* is Paul's theme in this passage:

> All this is from God, who reconciled us to himself through Christ and gave us the ministry of reconciliation: that God was reconciling the world to himself in Christ, not counting men's sins against them. And he has committed to us the message of reconciliation. We are therefore Christ's ambassadors, as though God were making his appeal through us. We implore you on Christ's behalf: Be reconciled to God. God made him who had no sin to be sin for us, so that in him we might become the righteousness of God. (2 Cor. 5:18-21)

Variations on the word *reconcile* are used five times in those few verses. Paul mentions, for example, "the ministry of reconciliation" (v. 18). That is his description of the evangelistic task. "The message of reconciliation" (v. 19) refers to the gospel message. This is how Scripture characterizes the gospel: it is a message of reconciliation. The duty of every minister of the gospel is to tell sinners how they can be reconciled to God. The duty of every follower of Christ is to receive Christ's forgiveness as the means for right standing with God.

God has a way by which He can accomplish the very thing that seems so completely impossible. There *is* a way to satisfy His justice without damning the sinner. He can both fulfill His promise of vengeance against sin and reconcile sinners. He can remain just while justifying the ungodly.[44] "Loving kindness and truth have met together; righteousness and peace have kissed each other."[45] This plan for the sinner's reconciliation is both initiated and obtained on the sinner's behalf wholly by God. The redeemed person contributes nothing of any merit whatsoever to the process. Paul says this clearly: "Now all these things are from God, who reconciled us to Himself through Christ."[46]

The relationship between God and the sinner is *never* restored because the sinner decides to change his ways and make amends with God.[47] No sinner ever would or could take such a step toward God. The sinner is in total bondage to sin, morally unable to love or obey God; he is willfully at enmity with Him.[48] Furthermore, as stated before, no sinner could possibly do enough to satisfy the demands of God's perfect righteousness. Sinners who think they deserve God's favor only compound their sin with self-righteousness. Their baseless hope of earning divine merit is actually a further insult to the infinite holiness of God, whose only standard is an absolute perfection unattainable by fallen humanity. Self-reformation is not possible. A mere act of the will cannot end a sinner's rebellion against God. "To suppose that any sinner could or would choose to restore a right relationship with God is to grossly underestimate the bondage of sin and its power over the sinner's will. Besides, the greatest impediment to our salvation is not even our hostility against God. It is *His* wrath against us."[49] God Himself must be the initiator and author of all reconciliation.

Yet God is not at all a reluctant Savior. It was He who came seeking Adam and Eve after they fell.[50] It was He who sought His wayward people and pleaded with them to repent and receive His salvation. It was God weeping through the tears of Jeremiah for His sinful people.[51] It was God who was depicted in the story of Hosea going into the slave prostitute market and bringing His unfaithful, sin-stained wife back and treating her with love as if she were a chaste, virgin bride.[52]

McArthur writes:

This is the good news about forgiveness— "namely, that God was in Christ reconciling the world to Himself, not counting their trespasses against them" (2 Cor. 5:19). There *is* a way for sinners to be reconciled to God. Through the atoning work of Christ, God Himself has accomplished what seemed impossible. The enmity can be removed, the sin forgiven, and the fellowship restored—by God Himself, not by the sinner. That is what the gospel message proclaims. ... This is the distinctive of Christian forgiveness. Every manmade religion ever concocted teaches that there is something the sinner must do in order to appease God. Biblical Christianity alone teaches that God has supplied on the sinner's behalf all the merit that is necessary to please Him.[53]

The Cross of Christ

Here, then, are the basic truths underlying the Christian doctrine of forgiveness: God is the one who must accomplish forgiveness of sins; it is not possible for the sinner to earn his way back into God's favor. Also, if God is going to show mercy to sinners, He cannot do so in a way that violates His perfect justice. He has sworn to punish the guilty, and that oath must be fulfilled; otherwise, justice is not satisfied. So, until God's wrath against the guilty is fully measured out, forgiveness remains an impossible violation of divine righteousness, and no one can be reconciled to God.

The wrath of God against sin therefore poses the biggest obstacle of all to any sinner's forgiveness. Divine grace cannot be thought of as a sort of benign forbearance, by which God simply excuses sin and looks the other way—as if grace involved a lowering of the divine standard in order to accommodate what is unholy. So how does God reconcile sinners to Himself? On what grounds can He extend forgiveness to sinners? Here we are brought face to face with the need for atonement. If God's wrath is to be satisfied, if God is going to *be propitiated* to the sinner, a suitable atonement is required. God must fulfill the demands of justice by pouring out His wrath on a substitute. Someone must bear the sinner's punishment vicariously.

And that is precisely what happened at the cross of Christ. Paul encapsulates the whole gospel in one simple statement in 2 Corinthians 5:21: "He made Him who knew no sin to be sin on our behalf, so that we might become the righteousness of God in Him." This profound truth is the key to understanding divine forgiveness: God made the sinless Christ to be sin on our behalf, so that we might become in Him the very righteousness of God.

Substitution

First, the Cross of Christ speaks of substitution. It means that Christ died *our* death. He bore the punishment for *our* sin. He Himself suffered and satisfied the wrath of God that we deserved. Though Christ perfectly obeyed God's law, the Father treated Christ like a sinner and punished him for all the sins of all who would believe, treating them as righteous and giving them credit for what Christ did.

He substituted His Son, Jesus, for all men before the bar of judgment. He bore their guilt and suffered punishment in their place. And the true nature of the suffering He sustained was infinitely more than the humiliation and nails and flogging that accompanied His crucifixion. He received the full weight of God's wrath against sin.

MacArthur elaborates:

> In other words, as Christ hung on the cross bearing others' sins, God the Father poured out on His own sinless Son every ounce of divine fury against sin. That explains Christ's cry at the ninth hour, "'Eloi, Eloi, lama sabachthani?' which is translated, 'My God, my God, why hast Thou forsaken me?'" (Mark 15:34). There's a very real sense in which God the Father *did* forsake the Son—judicially. As Christ hung there, God was discharging against

His own Son the unrestrained fullness of His
fierce wrath and displeasure against our sin![54]

Astonishing as this may seem to fallen humanity, God
the Father heaped punishment on His own Son for guilt that
rightfully belonged to others! Yet, this is the clear teaching of
Scripture. The apostle Peter wrote, "He Himself bore our sins
in His body on the cross, that we might die to sin and live to
righteousness."[55] Isaiah 53:4-6 prophesies:

> Surely he took up our infirmities and carried
> our sorrows, yet we considered him stricken by
> God, smitten by him, and afflicted.
>
> But he was pierced for our transgressions, he
> was crushed for our iniquities;
>
> the punishment that brought us peace was upon
> him, and by his wounds we are healed.
>
> We all, like sheep, have gone astray, each of us
> has turned to his own way; and the Lord has
> laid on him the iniquity of us all.

In verse 10 Isaiah goes on to say, "Yet it was the Lord's
will to crush him and cause him to suffer ... ." The death of
Christ pleased God. Many times the Bible says Christ died as
a "propitiation" for our sins.[56] The word *propitiation* speaks of
an appeasement, a total satisfaction of the divine demands on
behalf of the sinner. This is a marvelous truth. It means Christ
paid the full price—the ransom—for sin on behalf of those He
redeemed.

Atonement by shedding of blood is absolutely essential to the forgiveness of sins. Forgiveness is impossible without a satisfactory, substitutionary sacrifice. The wrath and justice of God must not be downplayed in one's understanding of His forgiveness. Sinners cannot atone for their own sins in any way. A perfect sacrifice was therefore needed to atone for sin on their behalf.

This doctrine of substitutionary atonement is therefore the whole ground of God's forgiveness.[57] Apart from Christ's atoning work, no sinner would ever have any hope of salvation. The entire foundation of the sinner's reconciliation to God is the reality that Christ died bearing the guilt of every person's sin. He died in their place and as their substitute. He took their punishment and freed God to impute righteousness to them.

Imputation

The notion of imputation is important in helping to interpret 2 Corinthians 5:21. Imputation speaks of a legal reckoning. To impute guilt to someone is to assign guilt to that person's account. Likewise, to impute righteousness is to reckon the person righteous. The guilt or righteousness thus imputed is a wholly objective reality; it exists totally apart from the person to whom it is imputed.

In other words, a person to whom guilt is imputed is not thereby actually made guilty in the real sense. But he is accounted as guilty in a legal sense. It is a reckoning, not an actual remaking of the person's character.

The guilt of sinners was imputed to Christ. He was not in any sense actually tainted with guilt. He was merely reckoned

34

as guilty before the court of heaven, and the penalty of all that guilt was executed against Him. Sin was imputed, not imparted, to Him.[58]

The statement: "[God] made Him who knew no sin *to be sin* on our behalf" cannot mean that Christ *became* a sinner. It cannot mean that He committed any sin, that His character was defiled, or that He bore sin in any sense other than by legal imputation. Christ had no capacity to sin. He was impeccable.

So in 2 Corinthians 5:21, Paul's simple meaning is that God treated Christ as if He were a sinner. He imputed humanity's guilt to Him and exacted from Him the full penalty for sin— even though Christ Himself knew no sin. The guilt He bore was not His guilt, but He bore it as if it were His own. God put *our* guilt to Christ's account and made Him pay the penalty for it. All the guilt of all the sins of all who would ever be saved was imputed to Jesus Christ—reckoned to His account as if He were guilty of all of it. Then God poured out the full fury of His entire wrath against all of that sin, and Jesus experienced it all. That's what this verse means when it says God made Christ to be sin for us.

Justification

The 2 Corinthians 5:20 verse also contains the answer to the question of how sinners can be justified. In the same way that the guilt of sinners was imputed to Christ, His righteousness is imputed to all who believe. Christ was "made ... to be sin" because our guilt was imputed to Him. We become righteous by the imputation of His righteousness to us.

Christ dying on the cross did not actually become evil in order to bear humanity's guilt. By the same token, man does not actually have to become perfect in order to be credited with His perfect righteousness. How is the righteousness of justification obtained? Only by imputation. Just as God put our sin to Christ's credit, He puts Christ's righteousness to our credit.

That means each person's forgiveness is not dependent on some prior moral reform on his/her part. Every believer is forgiven immediately, just like the thief on the cross. No works of penance are necessary, no meritorious rituals. God's forgiveness costs a person nothing, because it already cost Christ everything.

When God looks at the Christian—even the most godly, most consistent Christian one can imagine—He does not accept that person on the virtue of the Christian's own good life. He considers that person as righteous solely by virtue of the imputed righteousness of Christ.[59] That is the whole point of 2 Corinthians 5:21. That is also what Romans 4:3 means when it says God "justifies the ungodly." That is the very heart of the gospel message.

How does one obtain this forgiveness? By believing. In Romans chapter four, Paul's whole point is that sinners are justified only through an imputed righteousness, and that imputation occurs only through faith. Faith is the *only* prerequisite to this justification. No work can earn it. No ritual can be the instrument by which it is obtained. In fact, Paul points out in verse 10 that Abraham was justified *before* he was circumcised.[60] So circumcision, as important as it was in the covenant God made with Abraham, *cannot* be a requirement for justification or a means to it.

36

This faith is a refusal to trust anything *but* Christ for salvation. It means the abandonment of self-righteousness and a single-minded reliance on Christ alone for salvation. It therefore involves a sincere love for Christ and hatred for all that displeases Him.

"For God so loved the world that he gave his one and only Son, that whoever believes in him shall not perish but have eternal life." (John 3:16) Trusting in Jesus appropriates God's forgiveness. He offers forgiveness and eternal life freely to all who will come to Him. "The Spirit and the bride say, 'Come.' And let the one who hears say, 'Come.' And let the one who is thirsty come; let the one who wishes take the water of life without cost." (Rev. 22:17)

Forgiveness Reconciled with Justice

In Christ, God's justice and His mercy are reconciled. "Loving kindness and truth have met together; righteousness and peace have kissed each other." (Ps. 85:10).These two seemingly irreconcilable attributes of God have been reconciled. God has reconciled sinners to Himself. All Christians are forgiven an unpayable debt, not because we deserve it, not as a reward, but solely on the basis of what God Himself has done for us.

That inestimable gift of free forgiveness becomes the ground on which all other kinds of forgiveness are based, and also the pattern for how we are to forgive others. The deeper one probes into this subject of forgiveness, the more one must keep in mind all that God has done in order to provide forgiveness for us. If one keeps in perspective how much God forgave, and how much it cost Him to forgive, one will soon realize that no transgression against a person can ever justify an unforgiving spirit. Christians who hold grudges or refuse to forgive others have lost sight of what their own forgiveness involves.

Father's Love

Love is at the heart of forgiveness and God's redemptive story.[61] In society today, much confusion exists as to the real meaning of love. Despite the world's confusion, an objective, universal understanding of love exists and is described in Scripture from Genesis to Revelation. True *agape* love transcends all of creation and is the supreme grace of God. However, the eyes and hearts of the world cannot grasp the full relevance or significance of such love. God opens the eyes and changes the heart, so that one knows the reality of a love that is of incomparable worth, yet is freely given at a cost to the Lover, and experiences the veracity of a love that knows all about its object, yet is impartially offered. Such love is not some esoteric notion that can only be discussed philosophically—quite the contrary. Such love actually existed in bodily form, lived among humanity, and ultimately revealed Himself through a single, supreme act—"But God demonstrates His own love toward us, in that while we were yet sinners, Christ died for us" (Rom. 5:8). Morris poignantly states, "When we see man for what he is, the wrath of God for what it is, and the cross for what it is, then and only then do we see love for what it is."[62]

Scripture not only expresses love in terms of action, but in a more definite and personal manner—"God is love."[63] An objective, universal understanding of love is Theo centric; it starts with God, ends with God, and describes God Himself.

Holy Spirit Power

The Holy Spirit, third person of the Trinity and the One who empowered David, Jesus, the early church, and all believers,[64] is the One who empowers the ability to love and forgive.

The Spirit of God is the Spirit of love,[65] which enables love to abide continually in the souls of His children. God commands love, for He empowers the human heart to love according to His created design, as His own Spirit of love works in and through His children. The love for God and love for others is the same love, and both testify to the transforming power of God in this new era of the kingdom.[66] The Spirit of love disposes the heart to do good in both attitude and actions: to be meek in response to injuries as opposed to an angry spirit; to be humble towards others as opposed to an envious or judgmental spirit; and to look after the interests of others as opposed to merely looking out for one's own interests.[67]

In the Old Testament, God is the subject in passages which explicitly connect love and forgiveness, whereas in the New Testament passages linking love and forgiveness, the children of God are the subjects, as they are exhorted to love and forgive like Christ. This switch in subjects associated with love and forgiveness is accompanied by the enabling Spirit of God working in and through the redeemed souls of His children. Christians are called in the present to abide by the holy standards of love and forgiveness associated with the future eternal kingdom of God.[68] The divine, indwelling Spirit of love enables God's people to love and forgive in supernatural ways like Christ.

God's forgiveness is the pattern by which we are to forgive, and the best model of that is Christ Himself who demonstrated the power of the Holy Spirit at work to accomplish it. The next chapter moves from the divine to the human side of forgiveness, from the legal work of justification to the process of sanctification.

FOR FURTHER FOLLOW-UP, PRACTICE, AND REFLECTIONS GUIDING COMMENTS

For each of the sections of the book, experiences, partial case stories, analysis, and study materials are presented for greater understanding and more thorough practice of the concept discussed. For each part, questions are presented to help guide your thinking and feeling processes for further reflection. I encourage you to pray and ask God to reveal to you answers that will facilitate further healing of your whole person.

The very first step in the journey is to acknowledge your need for the Savior. Chapter Three explains what Jesus has done to provide salvation and how you can access it. Trusting in Christ gets you started, and trusting in Christ is what keeps you going all along the way. If you haven't received Christ's free gift of salvation, (justification) my prayer is that you take that step today. That is the only prerequisite for continuing the journey in the manner transformation is discussed in this book. Am I saying there is only *one* way (to God?) Yes, that's what I'm saying because divine *Love* is the only way. If you read Chapter Three and missed that point, a second reading with that in mind would be helpful.

As suggested in the Introduction, commit yourself to a long-term journey to apply the change that God wants to perform in your heart. Getting to know God for who He REALLY is, is similar to getting to know another human being, in that it takes time. "Come near to God, and He will come near to you" (James 4:8). As you draw nearer with a sincere desire to change,[69] he will give you the strategy for jail breaking the imprisoned area(s) of your heart. Try not to become discouraged if the approach (timing and method) seems to be different from that of others around you. Only YOU can hear God in exactly the way He wants to speak to you, and orchestrate transformation. Change comes about through getting to know the Master, not through mastering a method. "Love the Lord your God with all your [mind and] heart and with all your being, that you may live" (Deut. 30:6 Amplified Bible).

Hopefully you are finding the material in this book helpful in your journey of getting to know God better. I sometimes hear people say, "I've tried forgiveness, but it doesn't work," or "I've already forgiven as much as I can forgive." Remember, it's often like peeling an onion. Core issues cannot be fully dealt with until outer layers of issues are first removed. Wherever you are in the pealing process, hopefully you can find yourself returning to the book for further self-examination. Maybe the first time through you can pick out some of the reflection questions below that may be particularly relevant to your present point in the journey. Perhaps in a few weeks or months additional questions will seem relevant. Write down you answers to the questions, and better yet, record a journal of your spiritual insights and practice as you go. Life with God is all about change. You should be able to look back at any point in your journey and be able to identify specific things God has changed for the good.

For readers experiencing an especially hungry or brave moment, let me issue a further challenge. Instead of asking a question like, "Lord, is there any unforgiveness in my heart?" try asking "Lord, *where* is there bitterness, resentment, blame, and the like in my heart?" Since the transformation and sanctification process never ends until physical death parts our soul from the body, assuming guilt accommodates continuous improvement. It really is a question of "when" not "if" God wants us to have a deeper layer removed. Experiencing "bad fruit" (negative, painful symptoms or behaviors) assumes a "bad root" (destructive source).

Ask the latter question above only if you're really serious, because the follow-up has to be "Lord, what do you want me to do about it?" Painful heart surgery may necessitate additionally painful adjustments to facilitate healing. Heart problems caused by poor eating habits in the natural, may require restrictions of diet to correct the situation. If love of food has become an idol, it makes the healthier choices and limiting quantities more difficult. Heart problems in an emotional or spiritual sense will often require changes in natural circumstances to cooperate with God's purifying and refining process. The verse quoted above goes on to explain further, "Come near to God and he will come near to you. Wash your hands, you sinners, and purify your hearts, you double-minded" (James 4:8). You may need the help of a trusted friend or counselor to discern some action steps for securing the healing God is doing in your life.

My past career as a software developer gives me a natural picture of a deep spiritual truth. Building software for computers must include a process of breaking the program. It is called debugging. It is said that the process of debugging, derived its name from a literal bug which had to be removed from the circuitry of a machine performing instructions to achieve a desired output. Finding and removing "bugs" in computer programs is an essential part of developing and maintaining well-functioning systems. Creating a good program involves trying to break it intentionally. A mistake in the program's code creates incorrect or unexpected results. A program must be submitted to a process of withstanding every conceivable condition of operation in order to flush out all potential errors. When an error is found, it must be corrected without introducing new errors.

Debugging requires a thinking process that assumes the program is broken until it proves itself functional. Our human hearts are like programs under construction which contain bugs (dysfunctional judgments from our broken world circumstances) that need to be discovered, corrected, and retested for functional use by the Creator. Assuming we are broken puts us in a more receiving posture for God's grace and truth (mercy and justice) to be worked out in our lives.

A caution is perhaps in order at this point. For those who may be prone to excessive introspection, these comments must be taken in balance with allowing God to perform the process of "debugging," refining, and removing layers of darkness from our hearts. For those who have a tendency to look *too* deep inwardly, please do not take these comments into a performance-based cycle of defeat discussed elsewhere.

Enjoy the journey beyond a bug-laden prison cell!

FOLLOW-UP AND PRACTICE FOR PART ONE FOUNDATIONS

As explained in Part One, the greatest offense we face in life is our innate sinfulness before Almighty God. This offense needed to be punished, but God took the punishment. This offense created an astronomical amount of debt, but God paid off the debt. God only asks one thing of us; that we "believe" in Jesus[70] as the One who took the punishment and paid the debt of our offense. Through Christ Jesus, God's requirements for both justice and mercy were perfectly satisfied. If we believe in Jesus, we are freed from the captivity (control) of debtor's prison.[71] But like the unmerciful servant Jesus used to illustrate unforgiveness,[72] the unsanctified part of our being tries to grab control and keep us from trusting in the only One who can save us from our helpless condition.

The cycle of offense described in the introduction has a number of common variations and applications. Life circumstances often manifest a "cycle of control" which imprisons us. When we succumb to fear and unbelief we feel "out of control" and behave in ways unbecoming of those "God raised [us] up with Christ, and seated [us] with him in the heavenly realms" (Eph. 2:6). Instead of trusting God with our identity and destiny, we try to seize control of our own fate and perhaps even those around us. Before long the expectations placed on ourselves and other people fail to be met. We lose hope that lasting change is possible. We become discouraged, despondent, or exhibit a diagnosable behavior such as depression, anxiety, or addiction.

In order to be a good Christian, we make attempts to rectify our predicament but failure returns because we do not allow God to be in control of the solution to the degree He should be. Again we feel "out of control" and fall into repeating the cycle.

This may occur many times before a breakthrough finds our soul resting in God. Then we can say with the Psalmist, "Truly he is my rock and my salvation; he is my fortress, I will not be shaken" (Ps. 62:6). God is given His rightful place when we can say, "My salvation and my honor depend on God; he is my mighty rock, my refuge. Trust in him at all times, you people; pour out your hearts to him, for God is our refuge" (Ps. 62:7-8). But so often we put ourselves through much needless pain before we find God as our Refuge.

Sometimes it becomes more comfortable to take on a "victim" role, than to take responsibility for change. When bad things happen, it is often easier to blame something else, or someone else, than to "own" a role in the failure. A person with a victim mindset often develops a pattern of arranging circumstances (intentionally or even unintentionally) to make more bad things happen so that their victim status can be confirmed. A victim stance can quickly turn to a predator position when controlling another person's behavior becomes necessary to manipulate for a purely selfish outcome.

Thus, it is possible for the same person to cycle between victim and predator, squeezing God out of His rightful place of Savior and Lord. The victim/predator cycle can allow a person to be controlled by someone, while simultaneously manifesting controlling behavior toward another person(s). Sometimes this can be even more aggravated by an intergenerational pattern that places a stronger hold on a person's inability to break free.

Another type of debilitating cycle is shame and self-rejection. In this cycle a person projects both the victim and predator role upon themselves. The wounds and hurts of life are translated into "false" guilt, self-condemnation, or self-blame. The person does not like themselves in a condition or self-imprisonment, so they turn on themselves in hatred and self-destructive behaviors.

Other examples of control cycles include poverty, (physical and spiritual) disappointment-motivated living, living in unbelief and mistrust of God, and performance-based living. Sometimes difficult to recognize, these cycles must be considered seriously when evaluating levels of honesty and humility discussed in Part Two.

Understanding and practicing forgiveness is a key to breaking the cycle of offense and as mentioned, first understanding what forgiveness is *not*, is an important first step.

Forgiveness is NOT:

1. Simple remorse—Being "sorry" is not enough. One can be sorry that something bad happened, and still not be willing to change their heart attitude about it.

2. Simply forgetting—One cannot forget what they haven't first remembered. Forgiving an offense involves first calling to memory the offender, the offense, and the hurt so that these all can be *intentionally* surrendered to God.

3. Simply excusing—An offended person does not have to continually excuse an offender's bad behavior. Boundaries and confrontation are necessary elements of relationship.

4. Simply trusting—Trusting another person involves the trustworthiness of the person's behavior. God can always be trusted, and His trustworthiness is not the same as peoples' trustworthiness.

5. Letting *time* heal—Time can only complicate the issue if the root problem(s) has not been properly dealt with. "Moving on" often involves some form of denial which can only make matters worse from a long-term perspective.

6. Letting go—For the Christian, forgiveness is NOT a mere choice to move away from something, but must involve consciously surrendering that something to God. The past cannot be changed, but it may need to be temporarily brought into the light so we can see what is being redeemed by Christ's blood shed to forgive the debt.

7. Just a feeling—Most of the time a choice to forgive comes before positive feelings toward an offender. An offended person cannot wait on feelings to determine when to forgive.

8. Reducing unforgiveness—Forgiving is not merely finding a way to reduce the effects of negative feelings (i.e. denying, minimizing, blaming, or dodging the hurt).

9. A one-time thing—Multiple offenses require multiple times forgiven. God forgives us as many times as we need it, and He asks us to do the same for those who offend us.

10. Waiting for (requiring) the offender to behave a certain way—some excuses people use for withholding forgiveness:

- The offense was too great
- He/she won't accept responsibility for the offense
- He/she never asked to be forgiven
- He/she will do it again
- He/she did it again
- He/she isn't truly sorry
- He/she did it deliberately
- I don't like him/her
- If I forgive the offense, I'd have to treat the offender well
- Someone has to punish him/her
- I don't feel like forgiving him/her
- I can't forget what happened

In Part Two we will discover "why" the approaches above fail the test of forgiveness. It should be mentioned here that one common behavioral thread runs through a failure to forgive—denial. By its very nature, denial is difficult to recognize in ourselves. It's easier to spot in other people, therefore, we have to allow others to spot, and point out, the denial in us. Denial hides itself in many forms ranging from simple denial to minimizing, blaming, excusing, generalizing, dodging, or attacking. Like the water in the river of "de Nile" of Egypt, denial flows in the path of least resistance. Our nature tends towards resisting change. Denying our need for change keeps us locked in the prison of dysfunction. If we want to break free of spiritual and emotional prisons while flowing through our existence on earth, we must get beyond "de Nile" and flow in God's Tree of Life, the Word made flesh, Jesus Christ, our crucified Savior and risen, reigning Lord!

Questions for Reflection Part One

Please refer to the Study Guide at the end of the book for the study questions in Sessions 1, 2, and 3.

Forgive Our Sins

Forgive our sins, oh Lord.
We don't know what we do.
We thought we struck the enemy,
When in truth we're striking you.

Forgive our sins, oh Father;
Forgive us one by one.
We reacted in our anger
And smote your only Son.

Forgive our sins, forgive us;
We've wounded you severe;
In beating down our brothers,
We've fallen in arrears.

When we tongue-lashed and we
gossiped;
We've slandered Love Divine
And we've cursed the One who made
us
By believing evil lies.

Forgive our sins, oh Father;
We don't know what we do;
For when we hurt our brothers,
In truth, we're hurting you.

Our criticism and our judgment
Have pierced your heavenly heart,

Forgive Our Sins

And we've no good way to finish
The wounding that we start.

Show us how to pardon
And how to make amends.
Through our hands bring healing—
Broken lives to mend.

Then we'll stop the vicious cycle
Of bitterness and hate.
And we'll cease to fight our brothers
To chase the enemy away.

For when we stoop to help another,
We minister to you.
And when we love our brother,
In truth, we're loving you.

Arnolda Brenneman © *5-27-07*
   email: brenfamily@ihsworshiparts.com

PART TWO—
TRANSFORMATIONAL HEALING:

A PERSONAL MATTER BETWEEN MAN AND GOD

In Part Two we will consider four elements to be applied in practicing forgiveness:

1.   Receive the gift of forgiveness Christ has already foregiven,

2.   Yield to God in forgiving (releasing) the offender and surrender the offense to His judgment,

3.   Redirect energy from blaming the other person to believing God's ability to change the heart, and

4.   Practice these steps as often as is needed for all offenses on life's journey.

From the divine aspects in the previous chapter, the discussion now moves to the human aspects of forgiveness.

CHAPTER FOUR

FORGIVENESS: RECEIVING GOD'S GIFT

God has done His part. The legal aspect of salvation (justification) once and for all accomplishes forgiveness for all who believe.[1] With this understanding, continuing on the journey requires collaboration with God on the part of the human. God calls believers to "work out" their salvation[3] through a process called sanctification. Here forgiveness becomes a "personal" matter; not personal in the sense of originating within a person, but personal in the sense of God's truth confronting the sinful, rebellious, and broken nature of His creation.

Therefore, we must consider sanctification and the role of the Christian in appropriating forgiveness. Several acts of God occur in a person before sanctification begins: the gospel call (which God addresses to him), regeneration (by which God imparts new life to him), justification (by which God gives him right legal standing before Him), and adoption (in which God makes him a member of His family). These events along with conversion (in which a person repents of sin and trusts in Christ for salvation) all occur at the beginning of a Christian's life.[4] After discussing these topics in his treatment of systematic theology, Wayne Grudem then states, "But now we come to a part of the application of redemption that is a *progressive* work that continues throughout our earthly lives. It is also a work in which *God and man cooperate,* each playing distinct roles. This part of the application of redemption is called sanctification: *Sanctification is a progressive work of God and man that makes us more and more free from sin and like Christ in our actual lives.*[5]

Grudem describes three distinct stages of sanctification. First, sanctification has a definite beginning at regeneration, and brings a definite moral change.[6] This initial step in sanctification involves a definite break from the ruling power and love of sin, so that the believer is no longer ruled or dominated by sin and no longer loves to sin.[7] Second, sanctification increases throughout life. This is the primary sense in which sanctification is considered for discussing the topic of forgiveness in the remainder of the book. Although Paul says that his readers have been set free from sin[8] and that they are "dead to sin and alive to God,"[9] he nonetheless recognizes that sin remains in their lives, so he tells them not to let it reign and not to yield to it.[10] The task for Christians is to grow more and more in sanctification, just as they previously grew more and more in sin; "Just as you once yielded your members to impurity and to greater and greater iniquity, so now yield your members to righteousness for sanctification."[11] Paul also says Christians "are being changed into his likeness from one degree of glory to another."[12] Third, sanctification is completed at death for Christians' souls and never completed fully in this life. Because there is sin that potentially remains in their hearts even though they have become Christians,[13] their sanctification will never be completed in this life.[14]

Sanctification requires cooperation between man and God. In explaining the nature of God's role and man's role in sanctification, Grudem states:

> ... it does not seem inappropriate to say that God and man cooperate in sanctification. God works in our sanctification and we work as well, and we work for the same purpose. We are not saying that we have equal roles in sanctification or that we both work in the same way, but simply that we cooperate with God in ways that are appropriate to our status as God's creatures. And the fact that Scripture emphasizes the role that we play in sanctification (with all the moral commands of the New Testament), makes it appropriate to teach that God calls us to cooperate with him in this activity.[15]

God's role in sanctification is a primary one.[16] Jesus is our example.[17] The Holy Spirit works in a Christian to change his life.[18] The role that man plays in sanctification is both a *passive* one in which we depend on God to sanctify us, and an *active* one in which we strive to obey God and take steps that will develop our sanctification. Grudem states, "It is important that we continue to grow both in our passive trust in God to sanctify us and in our active striving for holiness and greater obedience in our lives. If we neglect active striving to obey God, we become passive, lazy Christians. If we neglect the passive role of trusting God and yielding to him, we become proud and overly confident in ourselves. In either case, our sanctification will be greatly deficient."[19] Christians must maintain faith and practice diligence to obey at the same time. This book deals with some of the active human aspects of sanctification as they relate to forgiveness and greater freedom.

Turning from Fear to Faith and Forgiveness

People may know that forgiveness is a biblical concept. Somewhere along the way they also may have been warned about the physical, emotional, and spiritual consequences of unforgiveness. Maybe they are genuinely grateful for a God who was willing to take on human form and die an excruciating death that they might be forgiven of their sins. What then, is the reason so many people experience inconsistency between their understanding of forgiveness and their willingness to confess and repent of sinful responses related to offenses and ungodly beliefs which mire them in unforgiveness? Jeffress quotes respected counselor and author David Seamands with this answer:

> Many years ago I was driven to the conclusion that the major cause of most emotional problems among evangelical Christians are these: the failure to understand, receive, and live out God's unconditional love, forgiveness, and grace to other people. We read, we hear, we believe a good theology of grace. But that's not the way we live. The good news of the gospel has not penetrated the level of our emotions.[20]

The medical model of dealing with mental health concerns involves categorizing symptoms to formulate a label. Labeling depression or anxiety, for example, merely as an illness to be treated with medications to alter the physiological makeup of a person, can miss the importance of recognizing the person as a whole: spirit, body, and soul. Many mental health conditions often have spiritual and emotional roots, and research shows that even many physical problems are rooted in emotional and mental health issues.[21] Christian mental health treatment, while not ruling out the helpfulness of science, must seek to remove the obstacles that keep people from following Jesus with their whole heart, soul and mind.[22]

Some so-called "emotional problems" are not really problems with emotions, but problems with thinking patterns (including core beliefs) which trigger the emotions.[23] Emotions are neither good nor bad,[24] and they can be a powerful tool in exposing and clearing up thinking patterns.

The Psalmist's Experience

The Scripture contains many examples of persons who examined their emotions in helping to overcome disappointments, adversities, and embittered hearts. Perhaps no one is more prolific in describing the emotional turmoil of his inner being than David.

David, ancient Israel's second king, is a person who experienced great suffering in order to fulfill God's purposes for his life. The outcast of his family, David was taunted by his brothers and not even recognized as a candidate for king when Samuel visited their house. Though David served the king faithfully, Saul (who also suffered from depression) hurled his spear at David, causing him to flee for his life and hide in caves to avoid being hunted down and killed. David also suffered scorn and humiliation by the actions of his wives and son. He broke God's commands by committing adultery with Bathsheba. Then he committed murder in an attempt to hide the sin of adultery. When confronted by the prophet Nathan, David demonstrated genuine repentance before God. Although God forgave David, the consequences of his sin remained for generations. Through his son Solomon, a division in the kingdom developed into a split between Israel and Judah.

Out of the depths of David's acquaintance with suffering came the psalm, containing much wisdom, comfort and relevance for today. Many of the psalms David wrote reflected the loss and grief experienced by God's people. Many, such as Psalm 10, are also examples of how David responds to God in his heart. In Psalm 10, the first twelve verses describe affliction of the worst kind imaginable. David is oppressed and totally defeated by things completely out of his control. His loss cannot be corrected in any way known to man, and he feels helpless.

Then in verses 12-15, David turns his attention to God, and cries out to Him as helper, deliverer, vindicator, and One who is willing to act on behalf of the helpless. Verses 16-18 display David's heart of gratitude and praise for the mighty works of God. The expression of the human condition is clear. David's heart progresses from anxiety and depression to allowing his heart to be wooed by God and then to the joy of resting securely in God's place of victory.[25] Praising His Creator and acknowledging the truth about who He really is (vv. 17-18), David cooperates with God and his heart is transformed.

In Psalm 10 David writes almost four times the amount of text to describe the sorrow in his heart, than he writes to describe God's intervention.[26] As with many other similar psalms, David takes the time to explore and connect with the pain he was feeling. Similar to David, many people worsen their affliction and heartache by holding grudges, blaming, critically judging, or worrying about things that are out of their control. God allows David to emote and patiently listens to his cry. He waits for David's thinking to change and his experience to come into alignment with the truth. As in the example of Psalm 10, the truth of God may be one heart cry away from inviting Christ's forgiving, healing presence into a struggling person's health concern or broken relationship. Truth transforms thinking, actions, and feelings.

Receiving the Gift of Forgiveness

Knowing *about* forgiveness is not enough; one must *experience* forgiveness. To practice God-centered forgiveness, one must know the Forgiver.[27] A cognitive ascent to the truth about redemption helps to prepare the way, but a personal relationship with the Redeemer affords the intimacy needed for the act of receiving the gift. For a gift to accomplish its intended purpose for being given, it must be received. An act of kindness shrugged off by a recipient does not complete the purpose for a giver expressing love. A $100 check may be given to a family member on a special occasion, but unless the check is cashed into a bank account, the gift cannot be discharged for its intended use.

The transforming power of forgiveness must be received and experienced in the heart in order for the "renewing of the mind" to be accomplished.[28] A Christian's conversion opens the door (deposits the check in the illustration above) to the Holy Spirit's power to appropriate the miracle of God's free gift of forgiveness[29] as discussed in the previous chapter. As stated above, sanctification involves a cooperative effort between God and man. One of the gauges of maturity in a Christian's life is the ability to receive God's love and extend His love to other people. Frost states: "Being able to express and receive love is the true test of our relationship with God."[30]

Recognizing both the volitional and emotional aspects of the suffering of Christ in accomplishing forgiveness creates increased awareness of the depths of God's love. Christ acted in accordance with the Father's pleasure.[31] No greater love can be known. The type of suffering Christ endured had been prophesied by Isaiah and others hundreds of years before Christ came to earth. Christ knew precise details of the kind and magnitude of his sufferings,[32] including the excruciatingly painful death He would have to experience.

As discussed earlier, in order to atone for the sin of mankind (to satisfy God's wrath), Christ had to suffer. "Let us fix our eyes on Jesus, the author and perfector of our faith, who for the joy set before him endured the cross, scorning its shame, and sat down at the right hand of the throne of God. Consider him who endured such opposition from sinful men, so that you will not grow weary and lose heart" (Heb. 12:2-3). In his humanity, Jesus suffered.[33] He suffered temptation;[34] rejection, and betrayal;[35] hardships in ministry on behalf of others;[36] sorrow and remorse;[37] and the struggle of accepting the suffering in the garden of Gethsemane.[38]

Christ suffered extreme physical pain in the process of crucifixion.[39] Though sinless himself, He suffered the judgment of God the Father for sin.[40] In his death, Jesus accomplished the death of death.[41] The work of Christ on the cross provides the basis of forgiveness of sin.[42] Forgiveness of sin was the focus of the teaching of Jesus.[43] Jesus demonstrated his power over evil, performed miracles (not being preoccupied with his own suffering), gave glory to whom glory was due (His Father), showed great patience in his sufferings, refrained from returning evil for evil, and maintained a sense of mission through it all.[44] His suffering in death and His resurrection give meaning and hope in the midst of our suffering.[45]

Living from the Mind and Heart

God placed man uniquely in His creation as a *living soul*.[46] Job writes, "But it is the spirit in a man, the breath of the Almighty, that gives him understanding" (Job 32:8). Man is a spiritual being, and as such, spiritually sensitive to spiritual matters. "And if the Spirit of him who raised Jesus from the dead is living in you, he who raised Christ from the dead will also give life to your mortal bodies through his Spirit, who lives in you." (Rom. 8:11) As explained here by the apostle Paul, believers in Jesus Christ have a regenerated dimension of spiritual discernment that comes from the Holy Spirit living inside them.[47] The spirit of a person connects to spiritual matters through both the mind and heart.[48]

God created human response as a complexly intrinsic combination of volitional and emotional elements.[49] God views each person as a "whole person" (both physical and nonphysical). Many Scriptures mention the words, mind and heart, contextually as a dichotomy.[50] Although some Scriptures seem to speak of mind and heart together as the same entity, many Scriptures indicate at least a slightly different makeup of the two. Distinctions are made between functions related to thinking patterns and orientation related to core belief systems and values.[51]

The difference between knowing about and experiencing forgiveness (as discussed above) may also be related to this distinction. "From their callous hearts come iniquity; the evil conceits of their minds know no limits." (Ps. 73:7) Here evil conceits of the mind lead to a callous heart, producing the fruit of iniquity. Jeremiah 31:33 says, "'This is the covenant I will make with the house of Israel after that time,' declares the LORD. 'I will put my law in their minds and write it on their hearts. I will be their God, and they will be my people.'" Here the act of "putting" in the mind is contrasted to "writing" on the heart (a much more involved process, as etching into tablets).

This prophetic word spoken by Jeremiah is quoted by the author of Hebrews to emphasize the gravity of Christ's sacrificial work for the forgiveness of sin.[52] "By one sacrifice, he has made perfect forever those who are being made holy."[53] Jesus Himself quoted Isaiah in Mark 7:6-7, "These people honor me with their lips, but their hearts are far from me. They worship me in vain; their teachings are but rules taught by men." When teachings and exercises of the *mind* do not accompany a *heart* devoted to honoring God's ways, Jesus calls this hypocrisy.[54]

The modern world has taught us to seek a "scientific" method to resolve problems, but the methodology breaks down when applied to human behavior. Trying to reduce human interaction to objective methodology does not take into account the individual's uniqueness endowed by his Creator. Because of the intricate balance of mind (brain power) and heart (inner being), a person must seek for both to be transformed in the sanctification process,[55] discussed more in *Redeeming the Whole Person* section below.

Spiritual maturity involves a balancing of the mind, heart and will in life issues.[56] A person's spirit is active in both cognitive and emotional experiences. The human soul is the meeting place of mind and heart.[57] Engaging the mind challenges ungodly beliefs and helps enforce new beliefs necessary for transformation. Examining (discerning) heart attitudes, thoughts, motives, feelings, and emotions help reveal core beliefs which govern behaviors. Together, the mind and heart contribute to the "whole soul" in the process of sanctification (healing) [58] and living out forgiveness. Some consider the term *soul* or *spirit* to describe a third part of man, while others consider this in the nonphysical part of man's being. For a discussion of the Essential Nature of Man, see chapter 23 of Wayne Grudem's *Systematic Theology*.[59]

An important distinction must be made at this point. In describing a person's heart; the heart is not synonymous with feelings and specific emotions. Experiencing life from the heart is not simply doing what feelings dictate. Feelings-based living leads to foolish consequences.[60] Living from the heart means there is an inner directive that, if governed by the Spirit of God, keeps the person on a path that is spiritually attuned to who he or she is and how God is leading.[61] When people's hearts are focused on God, they see who they are and know what they are to be doing.[62]

The Word of God instructs that a man's heart is "deceitful above all things and beyond cure", [63] and all need God to heal their condition (save from sin). Isaiah 53:4-6 states:

"Surely he took up our infirmities
    and carried our sorrows,
    yet we considered him stricken by God,
    smitten by him, and afflicted.

But he was pierced for our transgressions,
    he was crushed for our iniquities;
    the punishment that brought us peace was upon
    him, and by his wounds we are healed.

We all, like sheep, have gone astray,
    each of us has turned to his own way;
    and the LORD has laid on him
    the iniquity of us all."

The heart that experiences Jesus is a changed heart; a heart where He resides and provides forgiveness of sins. There are many references to a transformed heart throughout Scripture. One passage is in the book of Ephesians, where the apostle Paul prays for the new believers in the Ephesian church. "I pray that out of his glorious riches he may strengthen you with power through his Spirit in your inner being, so that Christ may dwell in your hearts through faith." (Eph. 3:16-17) Faith in the accomplished work (of forgiveness) of Jesus Christ is the most powerful agent in the process of changing a person's inner being. God wants to live in people's hearts. When He is there they experience the freedom and power to be the persons He created them to be. [64]

Acknowledging the need and accepting the condition require a great amount of honesty and humility.

Honesty

A very familiar verse of Scripture is found in 2 Chronicles 7:14: "If my people, who are called by my name, will humble themselves and pray and seek my face and turn from their wicked ways, then will I hear from heaven and will forgive their sin and will heal their land." Contextually, this verse is found in the midst of ceremonies to dedicate the greatest temple of its time. Why, during these holy acts of worship, would God remind His chosen people of the wicked ways at the core of their hearts? God uses the term wicked to describe His most holy people on the face of the earth. How can this be explained? God desires a radical commitment to heart transformation. Genuine transformation begins with an honest assessment of man's desperate need. At the same time that part of a person's heart may be seeking after God and submitted to His will to some degree, other aspects of his life may be influenced by evil and still need to be surrendered to God's will.[65] As discussed above, sanctification has three distinct aspects: changed, being changed, and change completed at life's end.[66]

Although man is in right standing with God through justification, the sanctification process reveals a struggle to please God and do what is right. Paul describes it this way: "I do not understand what I do. For what I want to do I do not do, but what I hate I do."[67] Paul says to the Corinthians, "And we, who with unveiled faces all reflect the Lord's glory, are being transformed into his likeness with ever-increasing glory, which comes from the Lord, who is the Spirit."[68] The first step toward genuine transformation is being honest about the continual need of Christ's saving (sanctifying) power to change the heart.

Acknowledging the Truth

God created an orderly universe that operates in accordance with unchangeable laws. He originally intended for these laws to apply to humanity for their blessing. If people would live as God intended, and thus in accordance with the way the spiritual realm works, we would be blessed.[69] Since the Fall, the effects of the curse, resulting from disobeying His laws, also began to apply to humanity. When unregenerate people sin, they set in motion God's laws working against them. They do not have within themselves the ability to stop the operation of God's laws, and therefore have to pay the consequences of their sins. "Do not be deceived: God cannot be mocked. A man reaps what he sows." (Gal. 6:7) God knew how helpless people were, so Jesus came to rescue them from this impossible situation.[70] Experiencing forgiveness requires acknowledging this truth and opens the door to be able to glorify God and reap blessings of fellowship with God while living on earth.

God's covenant blessing is extended for transforming all aspects of the person.[71] Through the miracle of sanctification, God provides a way for the changing of the inner person. According to theologian Rudolf Bultmann, the Scripture makes it clear that "salvation" is not only for the future life, but is also for this life.[72] With the supernatural power of God working in a person's mind and heart, God's plan and purpose in forgiveness is realized by all who trust in Him.

Accepting the Heart Condition

The work of forgiving another person requires not merely mentally assenting to a need for change, but also motivationally responding with a will to pursue the change.[73] A heart of brokenness is the fertile soil for the seeds of forgiveness. This theme is reiterated several times in the book of Isaiah which says: "'Has not my hand made all these things, and so they came into being?' declares the LORD. 'This is the one I esteem: he who is humble and contrite in spirit, and trembles at my word'".[74] God's Word is the ultimate authority in the Christian's life. A heart of forgiveness is produced by a heart accepting its need for the Word of its Creator.[75]

The sinful "bad roots" in the human heart are very resistant to change. Change is difficult. Tolerating the "bad fruit" (sin and its consequences) is more appealing than expending significant effort to change the source (sinful bad root) of the brokenness.[76] The human tendency to resist change impedes movement toward godly change.

One form of denying unforgiveness may be expressed by people trying to perform their way out of it through self-righteousness. Although good works might make a good impression on fellow man, they are useless (for salvation) in the sight of God. From God's perspective, a person's good deeds are like a "filthy garment."[77] Christians may sometimes fall into a cycle the Sandfords call "performance orientation."[78] The cycle develops like this: A person keeps overly busy serving in the church and receives much affirmation and acceptance for his or her work. The person's spirit begins to ask, "Is this really working?" The person becomes disillusioned and his performance begins to wane. His work fails to earn the love he craves and once knew. He spirals into a black hole of depression and perhaps self-rejection. He thinks if he engages and does more activity, his painful symptoms will go away. As his performance improves and the praise from others puts him at the top of the world, he once again burns out and repeats the cycle all over again.

To some degree each person must admit that he is vulnerable to believing the lie that he must earn the right to be loved, which causes him to work harder and harder to perform. This performance can be rewarded in countless ways: the job promotion, the higher pay, the status, the compliments, the sense of well-being that comes with approval and acceptance. It may all seem so right, but if God's glory is not being manifested in the activity, His presence is not breathing life into it. It becomes a dead work[79] fueled only by self-willed passions and desires.

Receiving God's forgiveness requires a realization of our need and inadequacy.[80] But it must always be remembered that God required nothing of Adam and Eve before He initiated the reconciliation process. He came looking for them and questioned them about their fig-leaf covering before they ever acknowledged their sin.[81] God does the same for each person. Accepting the Gift of Jesus to cleanse from sins requires not only honesty of an unclean condition, but the humility to receive the help to become clean. That's where humility takes over in the process.

Humility

Honesty positions the mind (reasoning capacity) to receive from God, and humility positions the heart to receive in the inner being. The often-quoted verse in 2 Chronicles 7:14 might be summed up with the conditional phrase, "If my people … humble, pray, seek, and turn, then will I hear, forgive, and heal." The entire verse reads, "if my people, who are called by my name, will humble themselves and pray and seek my face and turn from their wicked ways, then will I hear from heaven and will forgive their sin and will heal their land." The gift is free,[82] but there must be a commitment to receive it. The commitment is demonstrated through repentance, which is also part of the conditional side of the phrase ("turn from their wicked ways").

If a person can humbly accept his condition as offender before God (and fellow man), then processing the offense of another offender in the same condition becomes more likely to impact the core identity of the person.[83] The humble truth is that every person alive owes such a huge debt to his Creator, that a lifetime of trying to work it off cannot even pay a reasonable portion of the debt.

Jesus told a story to illustrate the enormity of debt, recorded in Matthew 18:23-34. Known as the parable of the slave's debt forgiven, a king decides to call for closure of the debt of one of his servants. The debt is about the equivalent of five billion dollars. Serving the king the rest of his life would not make a dent in the payments. This creates a legal dilemma for the king of not being able to balance the books because the note he holds for a debtor is worthless. Aware of this, the servant feels bad about the circumstances completely out of control. Totally humbled, he pleads for mercy. The king has compassion on him and forgives the entire debt. Legally and morally the servant is set free.

This story illustrates the condition of sinful man in the presence of a holy God. As Jeffress explains, this story also shows how mistaken a person is to hold unforgiveness:

> Many people today are struggling with forgiveness because they are unaware that the "debt" they hold is really worthless. They mistakenly believe that there's some payment they can extract from their offender that will compensate for their loss. Understandably, they want vengeance. But the truth is that very few sinners have the resources to pay for their offenses. What satisfactory payment could someone offer you to compensate for...
>
> a child killed by a drunk driver
> a reputation slandered by a false rumor
> a marriage destroyed by infidelity
> a childhood innocence stolen by an immoral relative?[84]
>
> Refusing to forgive is not just a mistake; it is sin.

In the verses following the parable of the king and the slave's debt forgiven, Jesus makes the connection and offers a solution. "You have heard that it was said, 'An eye for an eye, and a tooth for a tooth.' But I say to you, do not resist him who is evil; but whoever slaps you on your right cheek, turn to him the other also." (Matt. 5:38-39) Like the king in the parable, Jesus taught that forgiveness is the only way to break the cycle of hurt and unfairness caused by sin. For a person to accept the truth that he or she owes God a debt that can never be repaid takes great humility. For a person to accept the truth that other persons' offenses against them may never be properly accounted for (in this life at least) also takes great humility.

Proverbs 11:2 says, "When pride comes, then comes disgrace, but with humility comes wisdom." A path of humility may not be the easiest path to take, but it is the wisest. The role of suffering and adversity will be explored more deeply in a later section, but it should be noted here that human weakness has a way of naturally creating an environment more conducive to exercising humility. Human weaknesses and inabilities have a way of deflating pride, and as such, make way for repentance.[85]

Repentance

Some question whether repentance is necessary before forgiveness. To answer this, an important distinction must be made between *receiving* forgiveness and *granting* forgiveness. The issue of repentance is vitally important to an offender *accepting* the forgiveness of a victim (as part of reconciliation). Reconciliation will be discussed more in the next chapter. An offended person *granting* forgiveness to an offender cannot place demands (such as repentance on the part of their offender) as conditions for obeying God and practicing forgiveness.

Although repentance is a necessary ingredient to experience God's forgiveness, one should never forget that God has made all the first moves to bring about that reconciliation with His creatures. That is why Christians should understand that sometimes the offended party must take the first step to restore a broken relationship. Repentance and confession (on the part of the offender) are necessary to *receive* forgiveness (from God). At the same time, they are not required prerequisites for *granting* forgiveness, from the perspective of an offended person needing to forgive an offense.[86]

The parable in Matthew 18, mentioned above, also presents a second servant who owed the first servant sixteen dollars. The first servant mistakenly thought that imprisoning and torturing his fellow slave would somehow enrich him, or at least console him over the forfeited debt. Yet in the end, he collected no more of what was due him than did the king.

Those (victims) who think they can demand repentance before granting forgiveness are operating under the illusion that somehow their offender's repentance will be sufficient to cover the offense.[87] The same is true in a person's relationship with God. Since every person alive is an offender,[88] there is nothing one could ever do to earn God's forgiveness. Is showing remorse or even genuine repentance ever truly enough to erase the stain of an abortion, a divorce, an affair, or a broken vow to God? Jeffress answers, "How silly (and prideful) it is to think that we could ever repay our Creator for the hurt we have inflicted upon Him by any act of penitence, much less uttering a simple 'I'm sorry.' Mark it down, circle it, and remember this forever: we are not saved by our repentance but by God's grace."[89]

Nonetheless, repentance and forgiveness fit hand in glove in releasing an offender from his offense. The offended person's willingness to take responsibility for any part he or she plays in causing the offense demonstrates a true heart of humility, shows the love of God, and opens the door for reconciliation in the proper timing.[90]

Forgiving To Gain Physical and Psychological Health

Yielding to God in obedience to forgive is rarely an easy choice. In her book *Choosing Forgiveness*, Nancy DeMoss challenges her readers, "It's possible that even after reading the Scriptures and examining the concepts we've explored, you still find forgiveness too painful and difficult to contemplate. Or perhaps, truth be known, you'd rather keep nursing your wounds and savoring your resentment than to release the offense. Either way you're just not ready to forgive."[91] For those who fall into this category, she then warns, "Your unwillingness to trust and obey God in this matter—even if it's more from exhaustion and self-preservation than from rank hardness of heart—will keep the atmosphere of your life contaminated with the poison of bitterness. You may not be conscious of its noxious effects every day, but it will cut off the flow of God's grace into your life."[92]

It *is* possible to recognize offenses as terrible or horrific and still choose to forgive. Part of the reason some find this difficult is because of myths they believe about forgiveness. Exploring what forgiveness is not, helps in defining what true forgiveness is. DeMoss says, "Many people who genuinely want to find themselves on the other side of forgiveness have bought into myths and misconceptions that have defeated their best attempts at following through. They have misunderstood what forgiveness should look like, feel like, and be like. As a result, they've found their journey to freedom frustrated."[93]

DeMoss shares four common myths about forgiveness: 1) that forgiveness and good feelings always go hand in hand, 2) that forgiveness means forgetting, 3) that forgiveness requires a long, drawn-out process and cannot take place until healing is complete, and 4) that forgiveness should always make things better.[94] Forgiveness is first a choice and the feelings follow, whether good or bad. Wiping out hurtful memory is not the object of forgiveness. God's grace can redeem the afflicted memory. The Scripture reminds us that affliction not only allows us to receive deep, rich comfort from God, but gives us a basis from which to minister that comfort to others.[95] By God's grace, a person can choose to forgive in a moment of time, to the level of his understanding at that point. And as he grows in his understanding of the circumstances that took place, as well as his understanding of God's ways, the forgiveness in his heart may likely go to deeper levels. Finally, not only may the results of forgiveness not feel better, they possibly will not *be* better. Unfairness and mistreatment by others are never guaranteed to go away.

CHAPTER FIVE

FORGIVENESS: SURRENDERING TO GOD

The Act and Art of Forgiving

The essence of forgiveness is yielding to God and releasing the offense. It is surrendering to God the right to reclaim debt. To "forgive" comes from a Greek word that means "to let be" or "to send away."[1] When one prays, "*Forgive* us our debts, as we also have forgiven our debtors" (Matt. 6:12), he is asking God to "let go" his debts (sins) as he has "let go" others' indebtedness. Since Jesus already paid the debt for the person who is trusting Christ to pay it, God will "let go" the offense (sin) and wipe away whatever an offender owes. His sin is "sent away"—cast away from him with no liability for it. Since God forgives the debt (releases the obligation) of the person asking Him to be forgiven, a person must release the debt of his offender(s), trusting Christ to deal with it, in order to allow God's grace of forgiveness to be completed.[2]

Jesus teaches, "For if you forgive men when they sin against you, your heavenly Father will also forgive you. But if you do not forgive men their sins, your Father will not forgive your sins."[3] It takes humility to receive this truth. Fellowship with the Father is directly related to how well a person forgives.[4] The essence of the Christian life is receiving God's forgiveness for our sins (offenses), and extending forgiveness to other sinners (offenders). God is more than willing to help his children forgive, because he knows a human's ability to forgive offenses requires supernatural intervention.

Surrendering to God the desire to judge the motives of an offender sometimes becomes a test of faith. A person must trust in the Lord Jesus Christ as Savior (debt payer). He must accept Him as the Son of God who has authority and power to forgive sins, to overcome death, and to make an individual into a new being. He must come to Him repentantly so that he becomes a malleable spirit in whom Jesus can work His transforming miracle. The Sandfords state: "Coming into the reality of forgiveness may require returning in prayer to the Lord again and again, each time old feelings emerge."[5] This does not mean that someone should reexamine the same offense once surrendered to God, but Christians should grow in the ability to yield the indebtedness of offenders[6] and accept that God is good and powerful and will handle the problem debt. Forgiveness is not a feeling, but feelings can reveal our true heart condition. When blessing replaces cursing, it indicates that transformation towards the "image of Christ" is being accomplished.[7] A heart of empathy and compassion towards an offender can be a fruit of the power of forgiveness.

Theological scholarship on the topic of forgiveness includes somewhat of a debate on whether or not one can "forgive" God or "forgive" oneself. Certainly "forgiving" God does not make sense based on what has been discussed so far. The creature cannot forgive the Creator.[8] However; anger directed at God is sinful and needs to be reckoned with. DeMoss goes so far as to say, "I have come to believe that, at one level, all bitterness is ultimately directed toward God. It may be cloaked in anger toward a particular person or group of people who have wronged us, but it actually extends far beyond them, far above them."[9]

A related debate found in the literature revolves around whether or not attaching "blame" is necessary in forgiveness. Some say that blame must be attached to a person in order for forgiveness to be possible.[10] Sometimes, blame is difficult to attach to a specific person: examples are loss from natural disaster, accident, or other uncontrollable circumstances. Some push the blame inward and blame themselves, while others may blame God for the hurt inflicted on them. In either case, this is sin and needs to be forgiven. Forgiveness sometimes involves confessing generally and later forgiving more specific words and deeds (as the light of God's truth reveals). A candle dispels darkness, but the brighter and more directed the light, the easier it is for the eye to see. The Psalmist encourages examining the heart "to see if there be any offensive way in me."[11]

Some of the confusion surrounding the concept of blame may be caused by an incorrect understanding of "guilt." Guilt feelings must be distinguished from true guilt. The Christian life is to be lived in accordance with biblical truth, rather than being guided by our senses.[12] God's Word is a compass that never errs, but our feelings may trick us. Our feelings can misguide us, even as the conscience can be wrongly conditioned.[13] The Scriptures teach that we should be fully persuaded (as to right and wrong) by our intellects (in our minds), not by our feelings.[14]

Another area of differing viewpoints is in the relationship between forgiveness and reconciliation. Forgiveness and reconciliation are two related, but distinctly different, journeys.[15] Much of the reason for the debates mentioned above is a misunderstanding of the distinction between forgiveness and reconciliation. Forgiveness involves first being reconciled to God (termed "vertical forgiveness")[16] and is not to be confused with reconciliation with fellowman. Reconciliation between human beings is the work done to restore right relationship between the debtor and one to whom the debt is owed. Wendell Miller includes this in what he calls "horizontal forgiveness."[17] Reconciling with God and yielding the debt (forgiveness) to Him is an important prerequisite for restoring a relationship with the debtor (reconciliation). The debt(s) must be surrendered to God, and then right fellowship with God, self, and other persons has the opportunity to be restored. This restoration and reconciliation process will be discussed in the next chapter. Some distinguish forgiveness and reconciliation by using the terms *personal* forgiveness and *interpersonal* forgiveness.[18] The discussion turns now to two specific areas of surrender.

Forgiving the Offender

The sin of bitterness and resentment causes captivity and imprisonment. Luke's gospel records Christ speaking of His mission as prophesied by Isaiah: "He has sent me to bind up the brokenhearted, to proclaim freedom for the captives and release from darkness for the prisoners."[19]

Forgiveness offers release to those oppressed by the sin of rejecting God and glorifying self. Yielding the offense to God and surrendering the offender to His judgment is the only way to free a Christian from making a "judgment" that causes bitterness and resentment.[20] Kurath writes:

It is apparent that the key issue that inhibits our ability to forgive (and the reason that we judge) is: DO WE TRUST GOD TO BE THE JUDGE? Therefore, part of being able to forgive means that we need to trust that the person who sinned against us will be brought to justice. Our hearts have built into them a sense of justice, and so we know the person should be held accountable for what they have done. When we judge, it is a subtle admission that we don't trust God to judge them and we then take the law into our own hands. We become an illegal, self-appointed court.[21]

But the fact is that God is a just Judge. Even though we may never know what consequences the other person will experience at the hand of God, we need to be willing to trust Him to work in that person's life as He chooses. We must have faith in God's faithfulness and ultimate goodness. Contrary to how we would do it, He is always correct and just, and He does it for the other person's best interest as well.[22]

"Judging" is not always sin. "The Bible talks about four types of judging, three types that are not sin (good judging), and one that is sin (bad judging)."[23] The three good judging types are:

1) the judging *Jesus does*,[24]

2) the *judicial authority* that is to be exercised corporately by the Church in regard to members of the Church[25] and

3) the *discernment* that we are supposed to engage in as individual Christians.[26]

The fourth type of judging that is sin involves formulating critical, negative opinions about a person(s) not based on truth.[27]

As stated earlier, negative "judging" is what plants the bitter roots in the heart and is what causes a person to have bad fruit in his life. This is a serious condition that requires God's grace, through the blood of Jesus Christ, to be set free from the influence of these bitter roots.[28] Forgiving and being forgiven by God are the cure. It is the only way that the bitter root is pulled out and replaced by a good root, which is the presence of Jesus in us.

The above is true even when the imprisoning, critical, and negative opinions are formed about oneself. Some think of this condition as a need to "forgive self." Whether forgiving self is a fitting description of the process, or not, practicing honesty and humility before God (which may involve confession and repentance for sin) is certainly the way to break free from self-doubt, self-condemnation, self-hate, self-rejection, and the like. A number of the Psalms ask the question, "Why are you downcast, O my soul?"[29] Lamentations 3:20 ponders a similar dilemma. In these instances of Scripture, the authors realize the error of their self-focus and turn to God for their salvation.

Sometimes weaknesses or shortcomings people see and criticize (and find most difficult to accept) in others are sins for which they have not repented themselves.[30] Jesus asked a question, "Why do you look at the speck of sawdust in your brother's eye and pay no attention to the plank in your own eye?"[31] We make planks in areas as divergent as personality traits, financial management, athletic endeavors, or issues on the job.

Sanford writes, "As Christians we have many undiscovered pockets full of grudges and unforgiveness. We have convinced ourselves we are clean, when in actuality we may be seething inside with intolerance, fear and hate—much of which is focused on the reflection we see of ourselves as we encounter other people who in many ways are very much like us."[32]

"You therefore have no excuse, you who pass judgment on someone else, for at whatever point you judge the other, you are condemning yourself, because you who pass judgment do the same things." (Rom. 2:1) The Psalmist requests, "Search me, Oh God, and know my heart; Try me and know my anxious thoughts; And see if there be any hurtful way in me, and lead me in the everlasting way" (Ps. 39:23-24 New American Standard Bible).

God Is Never to Blame

Many people have difficulty admitting they sometimes have anger toward God. They make mistakes, or they suffer because of the sins other people inflict upon them, and then they hold God responsible. "A man's own folly ruins his life, yet his heart rages against the Lord" (Prov. 19:3). Misdirected blame often results when people think what happened to them is unfair.[33] Questions like these are common: "Where was God if He's good and loving? Why did He let this awful thing happen? Why didn't He rescue me? Why didn't He do something about it?" This is sometimes the case when a child is born with a disability, an adult is stricken with a terminal illness, a family member is killed in a senseless automobile accident, or financial disaster strikes one's assets for retirement. The common question is, "Why did God let this happen?" In the Bible, God sometimes allows disaster as a consequence for sin, but bad things also happen because the world we live in is an "after the fall" world.

A person holding bitterness or judgment against God needs to be honest with Him by confessing and repenting before Him. Of course God is not guilty of anything, and it would be blasphemous to think He could be in need of a human's forgiveness. A person's anger and unforgiveness are his own. They grow out of selfish ambition and desire for control. "When unforgiveness is lodged in the heart, it is difficult to see any way God may be using the situation to bring blessing or to write wisdom into us. Afterwards, when we have achieved forgiveness, we can verbalize lessons learned and thank God for bringing us through painful experiences with a positive outcome."[34] Obeying God in practicing forgiveness demonstrates faith in a God who "rewards those who earnestly seek him."[35]

If forgiving a debtor his debts is accomplished through Jesus, persons will direct no blame toward God for what has happened to them.[36] Their ability to enter into worship of God will be free and fulfilling. Hidden anger toward God blocks a blessing(s) He wants to give. If forgiveness is complete, people's hearts will be open toward God and toward others.[37] Open-heartedness, not merely open-mindedness, helps people learn from their own experiences that God produces lessons of value in any and all circumstances of life. Romans 8:28 (NASB) states "And we know that God causes all things to work together for good to those who love God, to those who are called according to His purpose." This open posture of the heart invites great things for the whole person.

Redeeming the Whole Person

Sanctification affects both the physical and nonphysical parts of the human being.[38] Scripture teaches that sanctification affects man's intellect and knowledge when Paul says that we have put on the new nature "which is being renewed in *knowledge* after the image of its creator."[39] He prays that the Philippians may see their love "abound more and more, with knowledge and all discernment."[40] And he urges the Roman Christians to be "transformed by the renewal of your mind."[41] A person's knowledge of God (including an understanding that is more than intellectual knowledge) should keep increasing throughout life.[42]

Moreover, according to Grudem, growth in sanctification will affect our emotions.

> We will see increasingly in our lives emotions such as "love, joy, peace, patience" (Gal. 5:22). We will be able increasingly to obey Peter's command "to abstain from *the* passions of the flesh that wage war against your soul" (1 Pet. 2:11). We will find it increasingly true that we do not "love the world or things in the world" (1 John 2:15), but that we, like our Savior, delight to do God's will.[43]

In ever-increasing measure, believers will become "obedient from the heart,"[44] and they will "put away" deeds and thinking involved in "bitterness and wrath and anger and clamor and slander."[45]

Sanctification will also have an effect on the human *will,* the decision-making faculty. God is at work in a believer "to *will* and to work for his good pleasure."[46]

Sanctification also affects the human *spirit,* the nonphysical part of human beings and a believer's physical body. We are to "cleanse ourselves from every defilement of body and *spirit,* and make holiness perfect in the fear of God,[47] and Paul says that a concern about the affairs of the Lord will mean taking thought for "how to be holy in body and *spirit.*"[48] Referring to our physical bodies, Paul says, "May *the* God of peace himself sanctify you wholly; and may your spirit and soul *and body* be kept sound and blameless at the coming of our Lord Jesus Christ."[49] Moreover, Paul encourages the Corinthians, "Let us cleanse ourselves from every defilement of *body* and spirit, and make holiness perfect in the fear of God."[50] As we become more sanctified in our bodies, our bodies become more and more useful servants of God, more and more responsive to the will of God and the desires of the Holy Spirit.[51] We will not let sin reign in our bodies[52] nor allow our bodies to participate in any way in immorality,[53] but will treat our bodies with care and will recognize that they are the means by which the Holy Spirit works through us in this life.[54]

The biblical use of the term *soul* is primarily referencing the inner aspect of the person,[55] in contrast to the outer person, or the body. The Bible presents an anthropological view of human beings as being comprised of both body and soul;[56] however, Scripture stresses the person as a whole, described ultimately in relationship with God and others. [57]

As mentioned earlier, neglecting the emotional part of a person's being can have damaging consequences. Peter Scazzero's book, *Emotionally Healthy Spirituality*, describes how even pastors and church leaders are susceptible to over dependence on intellect to solve problems. The jacket of his book reads, "... his church and marriage hit bottom and every Christian remedy he tried produced nothing but more anger and fatigue. As he began digging under the 'good Christian' veneer, he discovered emotional layers of his life God had not yet touched—layers he had carefully tried to conceal from everyone. The resulting emotional immaturity had left him spiritually immature—and it nearly cost him everything."[58]

However, for Scazzero, realizing the critical link between emotional and spiritual health turned the failure of his dreams into the beginning of a journey that would forever change him, his church and his relationships. Pastor Scazzero diagnoses why even intense spirituality and all its activity can still leave a person empty. Out of his pain-filled experiences and the seven steps to transformation detailed in these pages, he pointedly shows how one can escape the lifelessness of unhealthy spirituality and experience a fresh faith charged with authenticity, contemplation and a hunger for God that leaves one filled up and overflowing instead of burnt out and exhausted.

Although this topic could be explored in much more detail, the purpose in this chapter is to introduce some of the dynamics within the soul (person) associated with unforgiveness, forgiveness, and the soul's Creator—while fully acknowledging the fact that the person as a whole, is created, fallen, redeemed, and glorified. Scripture utilizes the term *soul,* especially in the Psalms,[59] when focusing on the struggles within the heart and mind of the psalmist, though presupposing that the person, as a whole, is in relationship with God. One must also acknowledge the dynamic, inseparable interplay between body and soul, which is becoming increasingly evident in recent neuroscience and neuropsychological research.

Medical and Clinical Perspective

Recent scientific research provides overwhelming support for a long known fact that forgiveness produces health benefits[60] and is better than holding a grudge. The most basic, proven reason is that chronic anger and resentment constitute a toxic form of stress. The harmful effects of bad stress have been known for decades. Hallowell uses the term "bad stress" or "toxic stress" to differentiate it from stress in general. Life necessarily includes stress, like pumping blood throughout the body or maintaining your posture against gravity. What kills a person too young is not ordinary life stress, but toxic or bad stress.[61]

Toxic stress leads to a host of medical and psychological problems. These include increasing the risk of a heart attack, giving back or joint pain, causing headaches, elevating blood pressure, and/or reducing the effectiveness of the immune system.[62] Even if people have been badly wronged, they are better off finding a way to let go of their bitterness and resentment, justifiable though they may seem.

Discussed more in the next section, Scripture clearly demonstrates a link between following God's laws and being healthy. "Do not be wise in your own eyes; fear the Lord and shun evil. This will bring health to your body and nourishment to your bones." (Prov. 3:7-8) The law of sowing and reaping dictates that good or bad consequences will follow good or bad behavior depending on which path is chosen.[63] This is very true of forgiveness as discussed earlier. Sowing seeds of surrender to God will yield a harvest of good fellowship with God and man.[64] Sowing seeds of bitterness and resentment will yield the fruits of misery and strife.[65]

Releasing offenses is an important part of whole person healing from a medical and therapeutic viewpoint. Psychosomatic illnesses (negative physical symptoms created at least in part by psychological problems) often have a root of unforgiveness at their core.[66] For most of humanity's history, faith and healing of the whole person were integrated more than today's medical model allows. The priest would administer healing in a temple or place where healing could occur.[67]

Faith and healing began to move apart as science developed and the spiritual aspect of life was gradually rejected. Science deals with that which is subject to physical measurements and experimentation. Medical science limits itself mostly to what is physical, observable, and replicable. In this process, man's concept of the person has become fragmented. In this model, diseases of the body are the concern of medicine, problems of the mind are the realm of psychology, and spiritual problems are relegated to pastors and priests. Fountain says, "It is now our duty as Christian practitioners to bring faith in Christ and the practice of medicine back together as an integrated whole. To do this we must first recognize the wholeness of the person we seek to heal."[68]

In medical science a growing body of scientific evidence finds that thoughts, feelings, and emotions have a controlling influence over many physiological processes. It has been shown how stress, over extended periods of time, affects the production of the adrenal-cortical hormones, which in turn affect the functioning of many of our organ systems.[69] Clinically, doctors and health professionals observe how an inadequate response to the physical, psychological, and social stresses of life can cause physical pathology. Many so-called physical illnesses (e.g. essential hypertension, autoimmune disorders, chronic inflammatory syndromes, and even some malignancies), have a strong psychological component related to inadequately handled stress.[70] Stress also affects the immune system by inhibiting resistance to infections and suppressing healing and recovery. Many articles in the medical literature show how faith, prayer, and participation in religious activities have a positive effect on health and recovery from illness. The Bible, medical science, and clinical experience all confirm that each person's body, mind, and spirit are designed to be integrated into a unified whole.

Scriptural Perspective

In the Bible, the Hebrew word *yeshuwah* means both salvation and health. The Greek verb *sozo* means to save, to heal, and to make whole.[71] Jesus cares for the well-being of his people, for the whole person—the physical, psychological, and spiritual dimensions. This is expressed in the letter that the apostle Paul wrote to the Thessalonians. "May God himself, the God of peace, sanctify you through and through. May your whole spirit, soul and body be kept blameless at the coming of our Lord Jesus Christ. The one who calls you is faithful and he will do it."[72]

Scripture has much more to say about the wholeness of the person. Genesis 2:7 says that God took the dust of the ground and formed a person. He used natural elements to make arteries, veins, blood cells, nerves, muscles, sense organs, and all of our organ systems. However, marvelous as this creation was, it was not alive. The person did not become alive until God breathed into it the breath of life, his Spirit. So we are more than just a physical organism; we are a physical organism imbued with spirit.[73]

Proverbs 14:30 says: "A heart at peace gives life to the body, but envy rots the bones." This profound insight makes it clear that peace of mind has positive physiological effects. It also declares that, just as cancer destroys the body, so does envy, bitterness, and many other unforgiving, negative, or destructive judgments.

In the New Testament gospels, many accounts are given where Jesus demonstrates spiritual truth with physical healing and also links physical healing with forgiveness of sins. In Jesus' earthly ministry, he preached, taught, healed, and delivered people.[74] Jesus healed sometimes because of human faith, sometimes because of his compassion, sometimes because of a combination of human faith and Jesus' compassion, and sometimes because of his sovereign will. His healing covers the physical, psychological, and spiritual dimensions. His concern is for our whole well-being.[75]

The most important healing Jesus offers is restoration into right relationship with God. An example of restoring a person to wholeness is found in how Jesus responded when only one of the ten lepers returned to give thanks to Jesus. He said to him, "Rise and go; your faith has made you well."[76] This leper received more than the physical healing all the other nine received; he received holistic healing, a harmonious relationship with God. It can be seen here that Jesus desires not only physical healing for people, but also restoration of believers to complete harmony with God. Another example is when Zacchaeus received Jesus into his home. Zacchaeus' life was changed. Zacchaeus' relationships were restored—with God, others, himself, and his environment. Through his relationship with Christ, he found purpose for being and learned how to deal with material life, sharing with the poor. He became a whole person.

Jesus not only consistently preached radically extending forgiveness to others, he also practiced it. He practiced it when it was incomprehensibly difficult—as He was hanging on a cross.[77] The victim of gross injustice, His body wracked with pain, the vicious taunts of His enemies ringing in his ears, He gathered his whole being and cried out, "Father, forgive them, for they do not know what they are doing."[78]

Jesus did not keep the power to heal and deliver to Himself; He empowered His disciples to do it also. "He called his twelve disciples to Him and gave them authority to drive out evil spirits and to heal every disease and sickness."[79] In His great commission, He commanded his disciples under the authority He had to make disciples of all nations and teach them everything He had commanded them.[80] The healing ministry specifically includes forgiveness. In the gospel of John, when Jesus breathed on His disciples before ascending into heaven, John records powerful words from Jesus saying, "Receive the Holy Spirit. If you forgive anyone his sins, they are forgiven; if you do not forgive them, they are not forgiven."[81]

The Christian imperative to forgive those who have inflicted pain (mental, emotional or physical) on us is a call to imitate

Jesus. However, we are not called to imitate Christ in our own strength. As we yield our whole being to His will to forgive, He imparts His spiritual strength to us. The Word of forgiveness spoken *on* the cross is also spoken *in* us.[82] Our whole person is completed in and through the transforming power of Jesus Christ.

CHAPTER SIX

FORGIVENESS: TRUSTING GOD FOR CHANGE

So far in this part of the book, the following two elements in personalizing the practice of forgiveness have been discussed: 1) Receive the gift of forgiveness Christ has already foregiven, 2) Yield to God in forgiving (releasing) the offender and surrender the offense to His judgment. Now the attention moves to the third, 3) Redirect energy from blaming the other person to believing God's ability to change the heart.

Judging as Chief Root of Bitterness

In the larger scope of transformation and progressive sanctification, releasing offenses to God plays a critical role in preparing people's hearts for reconciliation and right relationship in church and community. The life of a community is related to the maturity of the individuals who make up that community.[1] The faith level of a community is as strong as the level of faith of the individuals who make up the community. The combined effect of each individual's sin nature makes dealing with offenses a formidable and insurmountable challenge without the intervention of God's redeeming grace. For genuine transformation to occur, there must be an intentional effort by individuals to seek vertical relationship with God primarily, and allow fellowship with God to govern horizontal relationships with other persons. In any relationship (or community of relationships), when each individual focuses on changing himself (and not his spouse or neighbor), the true transformational power of Christ is accomplished.

Jesus has the following strong admonition for those who insist on comparing themselves to other people:

> Do not judge, or you too will be judged. For in the same way you judge others, you will be judged, and with the measure you use, it will be measured to you. Why do you look at the speck of sawdust in your brother's eye and pay no attention to the plank in your own eye? How can you say to your brother, "Let me take the speck out of your eye," when all the time there is a plank in your own eye? You hypocrite, first take the plank out of your own eye, and then you will see clearly to remove the speck from your brother's eye.[2]

Kendall says judging someone else is actually uncalled-for criticism.[3] That is what Jesus means by judging. When Jesus says, "Do not judge," He is not teaching that wrongs should be ignored, but He is saying not to administer any uncalled-for criticism; that is, criticism that is unfair or unjustified. In the same way a person dishes out criticism, "it will be measured" to him. Kendall states, "The degree to which we resist the temptation to judge will be the degree to which we ourselves are largely spared of being judged."[4]

A demeanor of criticism comes natural for human beings. One doesn't need to read a book on how to develop a pointing finger. Seeing past what is wrong in others and being willing to be critiqued by others are practices commanded by Christ's teaching. A test of maturity is being able to **not** point the finger.[5]

Jesus addressed the matter of when we are right to judge with a question: "Why do you look at the speck of sawdust in your brother's eye and pay no attention to the plank in your own eye?"[6] Since Jesus is addressing the church, it should not be a surprise that so many of Christians' quarrels come from within the family of God. He refers to "your brother's" eye—meaning one's spiritual brother or sister, not simply one's natural kin. This verse candidly shows how we tend to get upset over small issues (the "speck of dust") in another person's life and yet so easily overlook the big issues (the "plank") in our own lives. This lack of objectivity disqualifies us from being helpful. When we lose our objectivity, we render ourselves incapable of passing accurate judgment (accurately forming an opinion) on another person.[7] Kendall states:

> Fault-finding, then, is out of order. Jesus' rhetorical question forces us to confront our tendency to meddle over what gets our goat. The fault we see in someone else is what Jesus calls a "speck"—a little thing that annoys us. But the whole time we overlook our own very serious problems. Ironically, the cause of fault-finding, or meddling, is the plank in our own eye that we cannot see. "Plank" is Jesus' word for what is wrong with us; it is the sin in us, the

evidence of our fallen nature. It is what makes
us so eager to point the finger rather than to
forgive.[8]

The planks in peoples' eyes cause poor eyesight; they magnify the specks of dust in others while simultaneously blinding them to their own faults. The planks in peoples' eyes focus on and enlarge the weaknesses in others, causing them to appear much worse than they really are. In actuality, it is their own weaknesses that are in operation, simultaneously magnifying others' faults and blinding them to their own faults. The act of fault-finding is worse than the fault they think they see in the other person. Paying sufficient attention to their own plank will keep people from pointing the finger at others or meddling in situations where they do not belong. It will keep them more accurately focused on their own forgiveness and reconciliation journey. It will also help them to "see clearly to remove the speck from your brother's eye."[9] This will be discussed more in the next chapter.

Forgiveness as a Journey

The doctrine of sanctification includes an aspect of future (beyond this life) completeness in Christ-likeness.[10] While living on this earth, however, the journey for Christians' sanctification is understood by two aspects: 1) being set apart by God as His children at the time of conversion,[11] and 2) a continuing "work of God and man that makes us more and more free from sin and like Christ in our actual lives."[12] For the context of this book, sanctification is understood both as a unique position in Christ and as the growth of the whole person in Christ-likeness—cognitively, emotionally, volitionally, spiritually, and physically.[13] The redeemed person demonstrates the dynamics of forgiveness in tandem with the dynamics of sanctification.

Many authors speak of forgiveness both as an event and as a process. Viewing forgiveness as a journey helps to emphasize the need for practicing forgiveness as a lifestyle.

The basics of forgiving are the same for everyone. When forgiving offenders, the offended person travels the same basic transformational journey to become right with God and his fellow men. Each person's healing (sanctification) follows the same basic pattern: practice honesty and humility regarding the human condition, confess and repent for rebellion against God, receive God's free gift of salvation, by surrendering to Jesus with mind and heart, forgive offenders, and try to reconcile human relationships wherever possible. However, it is also true that no two situations are exactly the same. No two people react exactly the same way after they have been wronged. Each person responds to God uniquely regarding the inner dynamics of forgiving the wrong. Furthermore, each person makes his or her own decision about how to relate to someone after the offended one is forgiven. Each relates to God differently in welcoming the supernatural intervention He has provided. While God's love is extended in equal measure to all,[14] each person fills in the pattern of the forgiveness journey in a unique manner.[15]

Lewis Smedes outlines three stages of forgiveness in his book, *The Art of Forgiveness*. They are: 1) We rediscover the humanity of the person who hurt us, 2) We surrender our right to get even, and 3) We revise our feelings toward the person we forgive.[16] Rediscovering the humanity of the person who hurt us involves correcting our skewed perception of the offender's actions and intentions. The lens dirtied by hate is exchanged with an image created in the likeness of God. As the mind is renewed[17] and thinking patterns are changed, feelings and emotions come into proper alignment with the truth.

Surrendering to God the right to get even clears up the difference between revenge and justice (from our limited human perspective at least). Smedes defines the two as follows: "Vengeance is our own pleasure of seeing someone who hurt us getting it back and then some. Justice, on the other hand, is secured when someone pays a fair penalty for wronging another even if the injured person takes no pleasure in the transaction. Vengeance is personal satisfaction. Justice is moral accounting."[18] Forgiving surrenders the right to vengeance; it never surrenders the claims of justice. For the Christian, these must be surrendered to the hands of a sovereign God who convenes a court of perfect justice and perfect mercy simultaneously.[19]

The Old Testament Tabernacle was a place where God took care of the problem of sin; it was also was a place where He met with the Leaders of Israel. Joshua conquered every city in the Promised Land by creating a Tabernacle at the walls of every city. God came, the walls fell, the land was conquered. Jesus fulfills all that is in the Old Testament Tabernacle. He is our Tabernacle. He takes thorough and complete care of the problem of sin in our lives and is committed to conquering every "city" in the Promised Land of our inner life.[20] When we surrender to His leading, He comes, the walls fall, the inner city (heart) is conquered, and we can't help but give testimony to what God has done in us.[21] When enough people in a city have repented, the whole city becomes a Tabernacle of God.

When Jesus comes again, by His presence He will create a Tabernacle throughout the whole earth and all evil will be banished. Then the Scripture will come true, that "Now the dwelling (or Tabernacle) of God is with men, and He will live with them. They will be His people, and God Himself will be with them and be their God. He will wipe away every tear from their eyes. There will be no more death or mourning or crying or pain, for the old order of things has passed away." He who was seated on the throne said, "I am making everything new."[22] Forgiveness is the vehicle through which we experience this Tabernacle journey.

Some use the illustration of peeling an onion to describe the journey of transformation.[23] Each layer brings fresh tears. Reaching the core (root) of a problem cannot be achieved without first removing the outer layers. More knowledge yields deeper revelation. "For with much wisdom comes much sorrow; the more knowledge, the more grief."[24] Motivations of the heart are often deeply hidden. Proverbs states: "The purposes of a man's heart are deep waters."[25]

Engaging the Pain

No magic method exists to peel an onion without tears. It has been said that God is not the great magician—He is the great physician. People typically seek the quickest way out of pain. God's healing (sanctification) process through forgiveness allows for no shortcuts.[26] Physical pain demands immediate attention and often turns the focus toward God for healing. Likewise, emotional pain should trigger seeking God's redemption in the middle of the heartache. Friesen et.al. states, "God does His work in us, pointing us toward wholeness, even while we are in pain. But it is not simply His work; it is our work too. It takes maturity and tenacity on our part to achieve wholeness, and that means persistently dealing with our pain."[27]

Scripture does not teach freedom from adversity (or pain) as a goal for the Christian life.[28] In fact, an often-quoted passage in 2 Corinthians 12 describes how the apostle Paul learned a key lesson. When he was stuck with a tormenting problem which did not go away, even though he pleaded with the Lord three times, he received a surprising answer: God works through weakness. What a profound discovery. He learned to *delight* in "weaknesses, in insults, in hardships, in persecutions, and in difficulties."[29] The good news of the gospel is that God wants to be with each person He created in the middle of his struggles.[30] That is precisely when He exercises His strength in the person.[31] Paul learned to let God be in charge and to stop asking God to end his hardship. God's strength flowed through him because Paul stopped trying to be in control. He yielded to God, and God was able to use him for His glory. Paul could *delight* in suffering because he found it was an opportunity for God's strength to work through him. God's amazing power seems to flow most strongly when a person appears the weakest.

Central to the Christian experience is an unchanging belief that God is at work in all things for the good of those who love Him;[32] that means even things that cause offense. He is particularly at work in the believer when he is stuck in pain that seems to be endless and meaningless. Friesen et.al. explains that the time-honored approach to Christians processing pain that leads to wholeness involves their own activity as well as God's:

His work in us is to bring redemption to all of the
traumas that have broken us, and our work is to
strive for maturity as we progress to wholeness.
The word "redemption" is sometimes difficult
to understand, simply because it is used in so
many contexts. Here is the way it is used in
The Life Model: Redemption is God bringing
good out of bad, leading us to wholeness,
and the experience of God's amazing power.
Redemption means that out of our greatest pain
can come our most profound personal mission
in life.[33]

The biblical understanding of wholeness is linked to a
person's ability to embrace pain. This is described in the first
chapter of James. The Christian is instructed to consider it *pure*
joy whenever he is in the middle of suffering (adversity or "trials
of every kind"), because that will lead to wholeness. Suffering
tests faith and builds endurance, so that each can be mature and
complete—not divided, but whole. James cautions that each
must ask God for wisdom during this stormy process. It takes
total faith to believe that God will bring his children through
the storms, or they will be unable to "receive anything" from
God; without total faith in God they remain "double-minded"
divided.[34]

Friesen et.al. comments on the James one passage as follows:
"Wholeness comes as we let Him lead us through the storms. We
are to welcome suffering because it brings down the walls in
our fragmented life so that we can become mature and complete
(v. 4). It is God's intent to bring redemption to the wounded

and fragmented places in our lives so that our weaknesses can be transformed into God's strength working through us.[35] That can happen when we honestly address our pain."[36] Suffering can lead to being "mature and complete, not lacking anything"[37] if a person embraces it. It will take endurance and time, but the benefits are well worth it.

Paul writes to the Ephesians: "In your anger do not sin": Do not let the sun go down while you are still angry, and do not give the devil a foothold."[38] Anger, like other emotions, is not in itself sinful.[39] Unrighteous anger is a messenger that indicates a deeper painful root like bitterness or resentment.[40] Anger "management" techniques will not eradicate the root. The discussion now turns to how to correct the tendency to allow the negative roots to gain a "foothold."

Breaking Bondages

Forgiveness becomes especially difficult to achieve when a pervading attitude of unforgiveness manifests through a root of one's nature—when it has become built in (often times unknowingly) as a practiced way of life, generational pattern, or cultural norm. We all sin.[41] The author of Hebrews describes it as a "bitter root" which has the capacity to defile others by its lack of grace. "See to it that no one misses the grace of God and that no bitter root grows up to cause trouble and defile many."[42]

A helpful illustration is seen in the root system of a tree. The life of a tree is sustained by the soil in which it is rooted. Good soil produces a healthy tree. This can help one understand what a "root" means in terms of the spiritual and psychological makeup of a person. According to Sandford, "A 'root' is a hidden practiced way of drinking nurture or nonnurture, from God, others, ourselves, and nature."[43] Jesus illustrated this principle in the parable of the sower. People are growing in "good soil" when they "hear the word, accept it, and produce a crop."[44]

As one considers how the root of a tree functions, it becomes obvious that a tree is much more than what one sees above the ground. A tree sends roots deep into the soil of its environment to drink nourishment. If the soil is good, the root system is healthy and strong and the tree flourishes. Healthy roots enable a tree to hold firm to the supporting soil in stormy weather and give the tree resiliency to stay healthy in times of drought. If the soil is bad, the root system will be weakened, causing the tree to languish or to fall. Without a good root system a tree can easily be destroyed by disease or storms and does not have the capacity to thrive in times of stress. Jesus also illustrated this in His teaching about the wise and foolish builder in the seventh chapter of Matthew's gospel.

The spirit of a person "drinks" nurture and harm from the soil of their environment and from the flesh in a similar way as a tree.[45] A "root" is the way a person relates to others through their spirits, and through the structures built for the purpose of receiving life. This can result either in producing positive or negative fruits.

Roots formulated in earliest childhood become the nurturing patterns which shape character development.[46] Proverbs says, "Train a child in the way he should go, and when he is old he will not turn from it."[47] This principle applies both in a positive (godly) direction and negative (ungodly) direction. For example, a child who lives with parents who rarely give him affection and continually shove him aside is likely to develop that style of relationship as his own root behavior. If a person has not been lovingly and attentively nurtured, he or she will not have practiced habits of reaching into and expecting nurture from others. Rather, the person may develop "bitter roots," which, in this example, are practiced sinful habits of not giving or expecting to receive nurture.

Such bitter roots can reveal the "heart of stone" referred to in Ezekiel.[48] Healing (sanctification) requires that the bitter root (sinful response) be taken out—forgiveness being an integral part of that process.[49] Ezekiel 36:26 says, "I will give you a new heart and put a new spirit within you; and I will remove the heart of stone from your flesh and give you a heart of flesh." Even the best human parents cannot supply enough nurture to satisfy the "flesh" of a child born with a sinful nature hopelessly lost without Christ.[50]

Experiences in life, particularly in early childhood, can imprint negative attitudinal and behavioral patterns, sometimes so subtle that people may be completely unaware why they think and behave the way they do.[51] These bitter roots may seem completely normal to them—until they come into experiences in which their life patterns conflict with those of other persons. The roots can negatively impact relationships in both directions; causing persons to offend others and to be offended by others. Again and again, the practice of forgiveness must be exercised to further the sanctification process and remove the bitter roots.

These sinful roots can become so entrenched in the heart, they become strongholds.[52] Strongholds sometimes affect entire communities and cultures creating a need for corporate repentance and forgiveness. In the next chapter, this topic will be examined more closely. Since the Fall, when the first two humans on earth sinned together, humans have been uniting to break God's law. But no human efforts, even combined with the powers of darkness, can stand against the power of God. "For the weapons of our warfare are not carnal, but mighty through God to the pulling down of strongholds; casting down imaginations and every high thing that exalteth itself against the knowledge of God, and bringing into captivity every thought to the obedience of Christ...."[53] The power of the Cross through forgiveness is a mighty weapon to create breakthroughs.

Before moving on to discuss interpersonal relationships in more detail, one more topic deserves attention. All that has been discussed in this part of the book is held together with one unifying theme discussed next.

Connection to Love

God-centered forgiveness originates in, works by means of, and ends with God and His infinite and perfect love. Love is the supreme divine grace and is the most efficacious weapon against sin.[54] God's Spirit of love is implanted in the redeemed heart[55] and works in the human soul to bring about increasing conformity to God's will and ways. The dual dynamic of God's love at work in the soul and one working out one's own salvation in "fear and trembling"[56] with regards to unforgiveness is the process of sanctification. Authentic forgiveness requires a faith that believes that only the love of God can bring about a radical change in one's own soul, as well as the soul of the offender, through forgiveness—from God and towards others.

Forgiveness sometimes involves working through hurtful memories, sorting out the feelings and thinking patterns of the past, and struggling with the present sinful chaos in the soul associated with unforgiveness. However, the most important aspect of forgiveness is the creative, conforming, and communing work of God's love in the soul as it deals with its cognitions, emotions, and volitions. A God-centered definition of love and forgiveness establishes the foundation, structure, and essence of the dynamics of human forgiveness. Although the topic of God's love is most worthy of exploration at greater depths than space allows in this project, it must be mentioned as the foundation for a biblical world-view of forgiveness.

"For God so loved the world that he gave his one and only Son, that whoever believes in him shall not perish but have eternal life. For God did not send his Son into the world to condemn the world, but to save the world through him."[57] God's Gift of Love is His Son, Jesus Christ. Understanding and practicing forgiveness translates into receiving God's Gift, releasing everything that stands in the way of receiving more of His love (through progressive sanctification), and appropriating His love in order for His plan and purposes to be fulfilled in human life here on earth. As each person learns how to receive God's love and give it away,[58] the recycling is completed, resulting in God's glory and man's destiny being manifested.

God plays a central role in the dynamics of forgiveness as He works through His Spirit of love to overcome a spirit of unforgiveness. One of the main tasks of forgiveness is to restore and strengthen the wounded heart of the offended so that he or she can love, despite being sinned against. This also serves the godly purpose of redeeming the heart of the offender and gives praise to God's glory.[59] Christians have been reconciled to God through Christ, and have been given the "ministry of reconciliation."[60] In the next Chapter the discussion turns to the interpersonal aspects of forgiveness.

FOLLOW-UP AND PRACTICE FOR PART TWO
TRANSFORMATIONAL HEALING

Assuming you read Parts One and Two of the book, I now encourage you to make this a "personal" experience. As you read this section, invite the Holy Spirit to reveal truth about your heart condition. I pray He shows you areas in which your heart needs transformation, and gives you the grace to surrender to Him the rights of judgment. Are you perhaps so focused on the symptoms of a problem (the trunk, branches, and fruit above the surface) that you are unable to see the real issues (the hidden root structure feeding the behavior)? Are you perhaps trying to fix a problem by putting a different "spin" on the fruit (behavior), or are you willing to change the soil (surroundings of your heart) feeding the root system of the tree? Are you willing to simply stop trying to fix a problem and allow God to show you what He's already fixed (through Jesus) and what may still need to be fixed (your response to Him)?

At this point, I would like to address a common error in thinking. While categorizing symptoms and behaviors may be helpful for creating diagnostic labels used by professionals for treatment, these "labels" can often become obstacles to helping people see the "whole person" God made them to be. If a mental health diagnosis of "bi-polar" for example, is used by a patient to explain bad behavior, their desire to change the behavior can be diminished. When it becomes a surface explanation for deeper root issues, lasting change cannot take place until the root issue(s) is uncovered and addressed. Bi-polar, according to many experts, happens to be a commonly misdiagnosed condition. When psychotropic medications are introduced as a treatment, further complications of denial and other issues can occur. The so-called dual diagnosis of addiction, when treated with a substance like methadone, often amounts to substituting an illegal addictive substance for a much more addicting legal substance. Please do not misunderstand what I am saying. I believe medications serve a purpose for treating certain illnesses; however, dispensing pharmaceuticals that imprison peoples' hearts by stealing their opportunity for someday living meds-free, is an error far too commonly practiced.

We must also be careful about identifying personality traits and motivational gifts. Again, I am not knocking personality tests and gifting inventories (I use them myself). They can be very useful tools in discovering perceptions, preferences, motivations, attitudes, and the like, but when these discoveries become excuses for not being willing to change wrongful (sinful) behavior, they become counter-productive. A statement like: "That's just the type of person I am" as an explanation for questionable behavior often indicates a deeper issue to be explored. A person exclaiming, "That's just not my gift" may indicate a lack of willingness to change in a particular area where change may be needed most.

Balance is important here. To help avoid errors in thinking that we "have it together" in areas we actually need improvement in, or we "can't get it together" in areas that may actually be strengths in disguise, we should take more seriously our "common" condition of human frailty and weakness. From my perspective, there is no person alive who has a "forgiving personality." Every person is equally in need of the same divine intervention to be able to receive and extend Christ-centered forgiveness. In a similar vein, I believe it is unproductive to think of certain individuals as having, for example, an "addictive personality." If there is such a thing, then we all have it.

In my opinion, in order to be most honest and humble about our need to change and grow (as believers in Christ), it is more beneficial to consider ourselves as all having the same problem(s), perhaps in differing degrees. The apostle Paul in his letter to Roman Christians exhorts, "Do not think of yourself more highly than you ought, but rather think of yourself with sober judgment, in accordance with the faith God has distributed to each of you."[61] We are all prone to conditions that lead to symptoms being labeled as mood and anxiety disorders, personality disorders or psychotic disorders. Even organic brain disorders, such as degenerative diseases, lurk in our bodies as part of the fallen creation discussed earlier. Also mentioned was the inability to scientifically measure things like depression and anxiety, grief and loss, and the affects of trauma, abuse, and disability.

Downplaying the labels also helps Christian professionals and church leaders to not take ourselves too seriously in terms of our role in helping people through mental and emotional struggles. By emphasizing the process of sanctification through the transformation of the inner person, we can focus our attention more on the Creator behind the change, and less on the problems we see in a fallen creation. Rather than attaching characteristic labels to individual people, we should rather all consider ourselves having similar characteristics in varying degrees. We are all part of the human condition which is subject to depression, anxiety, bipolar, etc., and we all need God's grace in greater or lesser measure to overcome.

Human behavior cannot be reduced to a purely physiological phenomenon. Neither is a person's environment solely to blame for difficulties in making positive changes in behavior. Therefore, a strictly medical model of treating mental and emotional health issues will fall short of providing a long-term solution for satisfaction and fulfillment in life. Statistics reveal that the prison population in the United States is the highest per capita imprisonment of all nations in the world. A very high percentage of prisoners are repeat offenders. Without restorative justice our prison system will not be able to sentence and hold the increasing numbers of offenders. This should cause us to look more closely at what really works and what doesn't work in helping people truly change.

In a figurative sense, spiritual imprisonment mirrors society's growing problem of repeat offenders. Repeat offenders are trapped in a cycle of offense discussed in the Introduction. Trying to treat spiritual problems merely with a medical solution will not release a person from the cycle of offense. The jail break will only come by getting to the *heart* of the matter.

When the Scripture tells the reader to love God with his "heart, soul, and mind,"[62] that includes the whole self. The *heart* is a person's eyes for seeing spiritual reality; [63] literally, the heart is the "eyes and ears that know God." The heart is where understanding resides, and is the origin of spiritual discernment. It is particularly influential in shaping a person's sense of spiritual identity. God designed each person to be a particular kind of person, with characteristics uniquely his own. When an individual is living from the heart Jesus gave him, he is being the person God has specifically designed. Living this way integrates the *soul* where the feelings are included, and the *mind,* where the thinking takes place (Friesen et.al. 2004).

Trying to relegate a person to a box that is all good or all evil doesn't work according to Robert Jeffress; "If only it were all so simple! If only there were evil people... committing evil deeds, and it were necessary only to separate them from the rest of us and destroy them. However, the line dividing good and evil cuts through the heart of every human being. And who is willing to destroy a piece of his own heart? ... When we understand that the same evil that motivated our offender to hurt us resides in *our* heart as well, we're in a much better position to forgive."[64]

Edward Kurath describes a Christian's heart inside to be like a honeycomb as contrasted to a honey jar.[65] Having many compartments inside instead of just one, some are like "good trees" that produce "good fruit" and some are like "bad trees" that produce "bad fruit."[66] Kurath describes this further:

> We have a tendency to sin often. When we do, we plant dark places in our "Honeycomb," and these prevent us from following God's laws in those particular areas of our life. These bad roots produce bad fruit. When we repent and bring Jesus into those dark areas of our "Honeycomb," one area at a time, we are changed into His image, step by step. As He takes up residence in those particular areas, the

cursing side of the law stops. The good root of
Jesus produces good fruit.

God's commandments are a way of measuring
whether we have a bad root inside. If we
misunderstand and thus try to keep them with
our willpower, we will fail.

Even though we have the tendency to sin often,
we have the living presence of Jesus, and He
provides His blood to wash us clean every
time. There is no shortage of the blood of Jesus.
Through this provision, He has provided the
way for us to be set free from the sins that beset
us, by changing us into His image.[67]

Contaminated soil produces bad fruit. Redeemed (nutritious)
soil produces good fruit. Because the heart contains both good
and bad soil simultaneously, it receives the good and bad. This
struggle goes back to the Garden of Eden where man chose the
tree of the knowledge of good and evil over the tree of life. Part
of the curse was man taking into his heart the burden to discern
good from evil.[68] Part of breaking the cycle of offense must
include feeding our spirit being with the nutritious soil of God's
revelatory Word.

As discussed before, emotions like anger may indicate
a message of deeper root significance like bitterness or
resentment.[69] Using repression, the human mind can play a
major role in denying the true condition of the heart. The mind
often hides negative feelings to protect the heart from hurtful

situations. When an offended person does not handle the offense with forgiveness, the person also may not respond in anger immediately. An individual might say, "Oh, that's all right," or "It doesn't really matter." With good intentions, he suppresses his resentment and then later spends time rehearsing what he should have said to the offender. After a time of rumination, bitter feelings set down deep roots.[70]

Proverbs 10:18 says, "He who conceals his hatred has lying lips, and whoever spreads slander is a fool." Jesus expounds on the Proverb in Matthew 5:21-23. Anger, hatred, and rage do not "just happen." It's a progression. Judging (wrongly forming an opinion of) another person, ruminating, and failure to surrender to God are all elements of something I call a cycle of offense (explained in Chapter One). Anger (turned to hate) imprisons. Hatred seeks ungodly control. Hatred cannot just be left to "management." Hatred is a "fruit," that has a "root." Hatred must be yanked out by the roots. Since Jesus defines anger as simply calling someone a "fool," he is making the point that ALL of us are guilty of denying anger, lust, and other ungodly passions that can lead to disastrous results.

Christians are taught to be loving, thoughtful, and forbearing, so they often try to handle hurtful situations through reason and rationality alone. They erroneously think forgiveness can be accomplished simply by mental choice (without God's help), or that time and distance will heal all things.[71] They sublimate feelings and rationalize hurtful situations by saying something like, "He's always so busy; he just forgets." Denial of hurt may also serve as a convenient way to avoid healthy confrontation to help resolve differences.[72]

Denial also veils another aspect of forgiveness that can sometimes be overlooked in the Cycle of Offense (see Chapter One). The inability to turn to God when offended, is an offense against God in itself. You may be willing to finally let go of bitterness and resentment against the person for their offense against you, but having nursed the offense has made you an offender against God. Therefore, you are in need of God's forgiveness for your offense against Him. Sometimes it seems easier to forgive another person for their offense against you, than receiving forgiveness for your own offense against God. Honesty and humility before God is needed to acknowledge your offense against Him and receive His grace. Surrendering to God the right to judge your sinful response to being wounded will release your heart to properly surrender the original offense and offender.

Sometimes called sins of choice, empty wells, false refuges, counterfeit comforts, or idols of the heart,[73] people may develop addictive tendencies that can range from strong cravings to controlling behaviors. Addictions occur when we take common life experiences to the extreme. These include food (eating disorders), job (work-o-holism), drugs and alcohol (excessive use), sex, money, appearance, relationships (codependency), and even ministry (service to others). Whenever we are seeking comfort or fulfillment in a relationship or activity outside the boundaries set by our loving Creator, we are demonstrating our lack of trust in God to provide value and purpose in our lives. Not only is it necessary to deal with the immediate surface issues of addiction, but we must also identify and abandon false refuges in the heart where nourishment is sought in an ungodly manner.

If a person is honestly willing to recognize this condition with his mind, then the work of changing the heart can begin.[74]

In summary, most people follow one of two remedies to deal with hurt from life circumstances or relationships. People try their best to pretend things are better than they really are (denial), or they live to relieve it at all cost (addictive behaviors). Whether people deny or over-gratify, at some point, they become more painfully aware of their desperate state of human weakness and inability to effect lasting change without the supernatural presence of God working in their hearts.

For people to let go of denial or false refuge to face the truth about themselves is sometimes a fearful step. The tension between the Holy Spirit pushing truth up and a fearful mind pushing the truth down is known as anxiety.[75] It is the fear of the unknown. Part of a person is wise and wants to know the truth. Part of the person is foolish and fears the truth. The Holy Spirit reveals the difference,[76] and will only bring healing to those who humble themselves and are willing to be cooperative. As people give up their fear of the truth and trust God to forgive them just as they are, then they can begin to surrender themselves and learn to rest in the salvation of God's grace.[77]

Recognizing Unforgiveness

Unforgiveness lodged in the heart generally falls in one of two categories. The first type carries with it identifiable negative feelings toward a person(s) or situation. The second type is not definable with specific feelings, but carries a deep, well-disguised wound. Prayers of forgiveness can bring release for immediately identifiable sources of unforgiveness. Healing prayer techniques of various kinds can be used to identify more hidden sources of unforgiveness.

Is there someone (in your family or circle of friends and acquaintances) you discover you would rather not meet up with, intentionally avoid, or hope bad things happen to? Is there an incident you cannot get out of your mind? Do you feel vengeful emotions, frustration or anger towards someone?

If you answer yes to any of these questions, or if you have discovered "bad fruit" of unforgiveness through some means, it is probably time to proceed with this self-examination exercise.

Self-examination exercise questions:

> Who do you need to forgive?
> What did they do/say? (be specific)
> How did this offend? Hurt? (list specifics)
> When are you ruminating? (consuming fear or anger)
> Why are you ready/not ready to release/ surrender/let go of this?
> Where do you stand with God on this? (what would He have you do?)
> Where do you want to be/go on this? (next step)

If you are ready to forgive and you need the help of a sample prayer, see Appendix A for some help.

The following is a list of some of the common effects of unforgiveness. If a number of these are apparent in your life, you may want to seek help from a trusted friend or counselor to pray and ask God to reveal a source (or root) and what to do about it.

Common Effects of Unforgiveness:
a. Stress and anxiety
b. Self-inflicted condemnation
c. Lack of trust and love
d. Anger and bitterness
e. Perpetual conflict
f. Building up of emotional walls
g. Depression and hopelessness
h. Physical problems (i.e. chronic illness)
i. Sleeplessness or appetite loss
j. Wilderness in spiritual condition or relationship with God

God wants ALL the parts of your heart: not just some and not just on your terms, or in your timing. It's total surrender that He's after. He initiated the process of wholeness, completed His part of the work of salvation, and now only asks for your cooperation in transforming the heart into a tool to be used for His glory. Only through much prayer and reflection is the path to wholeness discerned. The Holy Spirit reveals truth to those who seek it earnestly. Now is the day of salvation. Seek God for your healing word. Intellect alone is not enough to discover, dislodge, or darn the sinful condition. Prayerfully consider some of the following questions. Practice "listening prayer" to hear what the Holy Spirit is speaking to your heart.

As you seek God for more revelation of His saving grace, I declare the spirit of Elijah to fall on you. Jesus said,

> "Truly I tell you, among those born of women there has not risen anyone greater than John the Baptist; yet whoever is least in the kingdom of heaven is greater than he. From the days of John the Baptist until now, the kingdom of heaven has been subjected to violence, and violent people have been raiding it. For all the Prophets and the Law prophesied until John. And if you are willing to accept it, he is the Elijah who was to come. Whoever has ears, let them hear."[78]

Turning from your condition (repenting) and allowing the "violent" winds of the Holy Spirit to blow the darkness out of your heart is the preparatory work necessary for the peace and "rest of your souls" as you come closer to Jesus.[79] This is the divinely masterminded strategy for jail breaking the imprisoned heart and escaping the pain of offense.

Questions for Reflection for Part Two

Please refer to the Study Guide at the end of the book for the study questions in Sessions 4, 5, and 6.

If It Were Easy To Forgive

If it were easy to forgive
Half our songs would not be sung;
Half our hearts would not be wrong;
Half our psyches not be sick;
Half our bodies not be feeble,
If we were able to forgive.

If we could live one day
Without a grudge, blame or regret
That would be a day not to forget.
Trouble breeds trouble; shame begets shame;
But all our excuses are lame
When we refuse to forgive.

If we really want to live,
We must put away denying
Of our own faults and failures,
And hear the voice that's crying
To be released in pardon
And freed in forgiveness.

We will have no true rest, for
There is no adequate jest
Or justifiable request
Used for plying bitter wares;
And for this we must beware
That we hold no unforgiveness.

If it were easy to forgive all wrong
There'd be no reason to live so long;
We would not face resultant storms.
But trust, forgive we must,
To ward off all the tormentors
And to have our land be blessed.

Arnolda Brenneman 4-2-10
email: brenfamily@ihsworshiparts.com

PART THREE—CONFLICT RESOLUTION: AN INTERPERSONAL MATTER BETWEEN GOD, MAN, AND FELLOWMAN

CHAPTER SEVEN

FORGIVENESS AND RECONCILIATION

A focus statement to guide the content of this chapter is as follows: forgiveness and reconciliation are inevitable experiences in worthwhile interpersonal relationships, stirred by conflict and testing of character in an irreparably (humanly speaking) broken world. Norman Cousins is quoted, "Life is an adventure in forgiveness." The personal matter of forgiveness (discussed heretofore as always being a cooperative effort with God) becomes an interpersonal matter because man is designed by his Creator to be a social being.[1] Sin not only affects the person and his relationship with God, but persons in his world as well. The sanctification of the believer includes a corporate aspect of the process.[2]

Persons offend and become offended. While the effects of taking offense and causing offense are processed somewhat differently for different people, these offenses are the essence of the interpersonal problems people face.. At the core of these problems is almost always some root of unforgiveness.[3]

Ken Sande, devoting most of his professional life to peacemaking, states, "Focusing on God is the key to resolving conflict constructively. When we remember his mercy and draw on his strength, we invariably see things more clearly and respond to conflict more wisely. In doing so, we can find far better solutions to our problems. At the same time, we can show others that there really is a God and that he delights in helping us do things we could never do on our own."[4]

Problems associated with conflict can be prevented if responded to in a biblical manner. In His word, God has explained why conflicts occur and how to deal with conflict. According to Ken Sande, in his book *The Peacemaker*, there are four primary causes of conflict. Some disputes arise because of misunderstandings resulting from poor communication.[5] Differences in values, goals, gifts, calling, priorities, expectations, interests, or opinions can also lead to conflict.[6] Competition over limited resources, such as time or money, is a frequent source of disputes in families, churches, and businesses.[7] Moreover, many conflicts are caused or aggravated by sinful attitudes and habits that lead to hurtful words and actions.[8]

Conflict is not necessarily bad. God has created human beings uniquely with natural differences. Disagreements are inevitable and can help create productive exchange. Some disagreements, however, come from sinful attitudes and behavior..Conflict should be seen neither as an inconvenience, nor as an occasion to force our will on others, but rather as an opportunity to demonstrate the love and power of God in our lives.

Jesus urged his followers to seek peace and unity. Knowing that God will sternly judge anyone who condemns or harbors anger toward his brother,[9] Jesus gave this command: "Therefore, if you are offering your gift at the altar and there remember that your brother has something against you, leave your gift there in front of the altar. First go and be reconciled to your brother; then come and offer your gift."[10]

Peace and unity are so important that Jesus commands a person to seek reconciliation with a brother even ahead of worship.[11] John teaches that people cannot love and worship God properly if they are at odds with another person and have not done everything in their power to be reconciled.[12] Paul also reminds people that their Christian witness depends greatly on their commitment to seek peace and reconciliation with others.[13]

Learning how to trust God is at the center of one's ability to do His will. The more a person understands God's love and power, the easier it is to trust Him. And the more a person trusts him, the easier it is to do His will. This is especially true when there is conflict. If a person believes that God is watching over him with perfect love and unlimited power, he will be able to serve Him faithfully as a reconciler, even in the most difficult circumstances.[14]

Peoples' view of God will have a profound effect on how much they trust him.[15] God's sovereignty is so complete that he exercises ultimate control, even over painful and unjust events.[16] The foundation for our trust in God is constructed of both God's power and God's love. He is not only in control over us; He is also for us! In love, He gives us life, provides for our needs, and never takes His eyes off us.[17]

Love is the Key

As discussed in the previous part of the book, honesty and humility are keys to opening one's mind and heart to the transformation process. As sanctification enlightens a person's inner being, one becomes more prepared to engage efforts in restoring broken interpersonal relationships. The key to unlocking the doors of forgiveness and reconciliation is love.[18]

A Christian worldview of love requires a definition of love whose source is divine. One might ask, "What is the love of God?" Divine love, as expressed within the Trinity, is the work of God to preserve and exalt His own supreme and righteous glory for His own enjoyment.[19] Expressed in relation to humanity, the love of God is His active, self-giving work in the human soul that enables one to worship Him, with unparalleled delight and satisfaction. Divine love, expressed and offered between human beings, is a work of God in the human soul that compels one to give oneself for another, regardless of the cost, so that the other might love God more deeply. The love of God is supremely defined and demonstrated by Christ's death on the cross—God paid the ultimate cost to redeem and reconcile us as a people for His own possession,[20] so that we might enjoy and be satisfied in the glory of our Creator and Redeemer. However, this divine love is often misunderstood when viewed from a human-centered perspective (Piper 2003).

Love Opens Doors

The Christian life is all about change: change in behavior, in perspective, in attitude, and most importantly at the root, in affections.[21] Divine love contends for the souls of others as it battles sin and stirs the heart towards holiness. All throughout the journey of sanctification, God's conforming love brings about increasing Christ-likeness in the redeemed soul, according to the Creator's intended design.[22] Upon conversion, the full beauty and power of divine love enters and embodies imperfect vessels wracked by the effects of sin. Love is powerful and is somewhat mysterious in how it impacts the soul. Love has the power to untwist, shape, and mold that which has been distorted and perverted, mysteriously and uniquely bringing about beauty from brokenness.[23] Furthermore, love has a way of healing deep wounds and restoring life and vitality to a weary and withered soul. God's perfecting love undertakes the reformational work of reshaping the soul so that the hatred of unrighteousness and the love for righteousness increases in intensity.[24] This redemptive work is completed in both body and soul in the consummation of history.

More could be said about divine love's purpose in the human soul—creating anew and conforming the heart to God's created design. Even though the love of God works at the individual level, there is a much bigger handiwork taking place in redemptive history. The eternal motion of divine love[25] is at work knitting together and building up a people for His own possession—the body, or bride, of Christ. Love is relational, exists only as it is shared, and does not diminish by being shared.[26]

Divine love knits together the Trinitarian community in perfect unity. Similarly, God's love not only redeems individuals, but binds them together to form the body of Christ.[27] The communal love of God that supernaturally produces the "love of the brethren" is "theandric in activity, Emmanuel, God with us."[28] In other words, God's abiding love knits together the individual members of Christ's body and perpetuates the love that exists between them, so they can live as one.[29]

The love of God not only binds His children into community, but also builds up the body.[30] A healthy physical body grows in stature and strength, as does the body of Christ. Every aspect of building up the body involves love.[31] Therefore, the building up of the body is understood as the building up of love within the body for God and for one another. Love is the foundation, the building material, and the building itself. Considering that love is the supreme grace and is the ultimate end—since God is love—this communal building up of love is the culminating purpose of love.

The portrait of divine love has been unveiled. As one stands back and takes in all the broad strokes of primary colors, love's divinity and supremacy elicits a sense of awe and worship.[32] Intense humility and a sense of amazing grace emerge as the cost of love is contemplated. Love's impartiality brings forth deep gratitude in the heart. The mysterious, supernatural, interactive nature of God's love causes the mind and heart to be dumbfounded as transcendent intimacy is encountered. One is transported into a radically different mindset as the definition of divine love is pondered. One is quickly reminded how God-centered love really is; God's love is the beginning and the end, and everything in between. Love is all about God, all about

His glory, for God is love. The portrait of divine love becomes animated and relevant as its purposes are illuminated by the gallery lights of redemptive history. The one who encounters the genuine work of divine love will never be the same. The eternal, uncreated love of God masterfully and creatively brings new life to the person captured by love, and then engages the heart in the sanctifying process of Christ-like conformity. The glare of sin fades while the glow of righteousness increases in intensity. The more one is overwhelmed by the vision of divine love, the more the heart is stirred to love others so that they too might enjoy the magnificence of such God-glorifying love.[33] The dynamic portrait of love produces a community of love, bound together and built up by love itself.

Jesus stated that all of God's laws can be summed up by the two great commandments to love.[34] God's love is the focal point of redemptive history and is manifested in His children's love for Him and for others. A God-centered perspective and practice of forgiveness and reconciliation must be rooted in a mature understanding of divine love. Jesus practiced what he preached and demonstrated divine love in action. He gave us a template for resolving conflict and pursuing reconciliation.

Christ at Gethsemane

The forgiveness and reconciliation journey sometimes takes a person through a Gethsemane-like experience.[35] On the night in which Jesus was arrested and tried, He went with His disciples to Gethsemane, a garden area in the Kidran Valley below the Mount of Olives opposite Jerusalem. That night, in fervent prayer and anguish, Jesus struggled with and accepted the purpose of God—He would take upon Himself the burden of mankind's sins. He would drink the cup of wrath of the nations. "This is what the Lord, the God of Israel, said to me: "Take from my hand this cup filled with the wine of my wrath and make all the nations to whom I send you drink it. When they drink it, they will stagger and go mad because of the sword I will send among them." So I took the cup from the Lord's hand and made all the nations to whom he sent me drink it."[36]

He would take into himself and become the sin of the human race. His struggle in the Garden of Gethsemane was not to accept having to die physically for mankind.[37] He knew He had come from heaven to earth for that very purpose, but He had never before felt separated from His Father. Sin separates. In His humanity, Jesus had to experience separation from His Father. "Who may ascend the hill of the Lord? Who may stand in his holy place? He who has clean hands and a pure heart, who does not lift up his soul to an idol or swear by what is false."[38] It should be noted that the Father's love was ever present even in the separation.

That spiritual death of separation from His Father by becoming our sin, thus unable to stand in the holy place of His Father's presence, was why He cried out, "Father, if you are willing, take this cup from me; yet not my will, but yours be done."[39] Becoming our sin, becoming one with us, was necessary to fulfill the law of God. The next day He would die as a sacrifice that we might be forgiven and brought back into right relationship with God. Therefore, in the intensity of that Gethsemane experience, Jesus went across time and space. He became us, in order to reap as we reap, and to reap for us the death on the cross that we were due to reap because of our sin. Praying as the God-man, He identified with us, entered into us, and became our sin. "God made him who had no sin to be sin for us, so that in him we might become the righteousness of God."[40] (also see Chapter Three)

The Sandfords describe the experience this way:

> When we experience the Gethsemane prayer in relation to a person or situation that needs our forgiveness, we are saying to the Lord: *"Help me to empathize with him. ..."* Such an honest prayer is intended to open our minds and hearts to feel empathy with the very person who violated us. When we enter into oneness with Jesus as He identifies with the sin of the other, the lines that separate us get blurred.
>
> ☐ We lose the sense of us (the good guys) and them (the bad guys).
>
> ☐ We commence to change our attitude about being the wounded party, or the noble martyr.
>
> ☐ We start seeing what we may have done to cause the other to behave in hurtful ways.
>
> ☐ We begin to sense what vulnerability in us drew harm from the other person.
>
> ☐ We may also recognize how we both have been affected by the sin of all mankind.
>
> ☐ Our prayers change from *"Oh, God, help me forgive that dirty rascal who doesn't deserve it,"* to *"Oh, God, we are caught in sinful reactions. Forgive us! We stand at the foot of the cross, both of us sinners, crying out for mercy."*[41]

A person can apply this to his marriage or to a close friendship. It seems to him that his partner is judgmental and continually wounds him with criticism. Yet, when he enters into the Gethsemane prayer with Jesus, he can respond with new perspective and understanding toward his partner. He may link that person's behavior with understanding of his own history. This will enable him to see the situation from the other person's perspective rather than only from his own. He can begin to respond in openness, honesty, and humility rather than with blame of the other.[42]

Releasing and Reconciliation

As stated earlier, a common mistake in pursuing healing of relationships is confusing forgiveness and reconciliation. Jeffress says, "While I can unilaterally forgive another person, I cannot unilaterally be reconciled to my offender. Forgiveness depends upon *me;* reconciliation depends upon *us.*"[43] Forgiving is not about reunion.[44] Forgiving is a personal matter with God that happens inside one person at a time. What happens to the other person, the one we forgive, is up to the other person. "And whether we restore him to the job or the place in society he had before he betrayed us and before we forgave him depends on reasonable judgments about justice and public safety. If we keep all these things—forgiving and judgment and good sense—in their right places, we can let the miracle of forgiving do its own proper work of healing and leave the restoration of the offender to other practical considerations."[45]

Forgiveness is both an event and a series of events resulting from its fruit. At some point in the journey after forgiving an individual, it is usually time to initiate another kind of event to knock down a wall that stands between the forgiver and a person who has been forgiven. Then a different kind of process begins. Sande describes this as follows: "After you demolish an obstruction, you usually have to clear away debris and do repair work. The Bible calls this 'reconciliation,' a process involving a change of attitude that leads to a change in the relationship."[46] To be reconciled means to replace hostility and separation with peace and friendship. This is what Jesus had in mind when he said, "Go and be reconciled to your brother."[47]

Being reconciled does not mean that the offender must become the closest friend of the person offended.[48] What it means is that their relationship will be at least as good as it was before the offense occurred. Once that happens, an even better relationship may develop. As God helps them work through their differences, they may discover a growing respect and appreciation for each other. Moreover, they may uncover common interests and goals that will add a deeper and richer dimension to their friendship.

Reconciliation requires that the injured party give a repentant person an opportunity to demonstrate repentance and regain his trust.[49] This may be a slow and difficult journey, especially when that person has consistently behaved in a hurtful and irresponsible manner. While it may be wise to proceed with some caution, one should not demand guarantees from a person who has expressed repentance. If the person stumbles, the practice of loving confrontation, confession, and forgiveness may need to be repeated.[50] In spite of setbacks and disappointments, for the Lord's sake, the process of reconciliation should continue until the relationship has been totally restored.[51]

Although reconciliation can sometimes take place with little or no special effort, in most cases it takes great effort and determination. This is especially true, for example, when marriage partners are recovering from intense and prolonged conflict. If definite, intentional steps are not taken to demonstrate repentance and forgiveness, one of the partners may doubt the other's sincerity and withdraw from the process.[52]

According to Everett Worthington, while some degree of reconciliation can occur without each partner forgiving the other,[53] forgiveness usually makes reconciliation easier and more lasting. A biblical view of this matter requires a Christian to pursue forgiveness and reconciliation regardless of how easy it may be.[54] In order to restore the damaged relationship, each must decide to pursue reconciliation to mend the perceived wounds of the past. Each must deal with his own issues of forgiveness separately and take 100 percent of the responsibility for his part in the problem(s) between them. After partners forgive, they can try to eliminate accumulated poisons in their relationship, and finally build positive acts of love and devotion into their interactions.

Repentance and Confession

In the similar manner that repentance and confession are keys in reconciling oneself to God, repentance and confession are critical in reconciliation with fellowman. Sorrow, remorse, and regret may accompany repentance, but neither can ever be equated with it.[55] A weeping offender in the presence of an offended person does not necessarily identify true repentance.[56] Repentance is not a feeling. A person may regret his words or actions, but not be repentant (e.g. Saul, Esau in the Bible).

Regret comes from many causes and may be mixed with true repentance, but real repentance comes only from the honest acknowledgment of sin.

In calling Israel to repentance, Isaiah (as God's representative), demands that she forsake her thoughts and ways, because they are not His ways—which He sets over against theirs. Instead, God insists she must begin thinking His thoughts after Him and walking in His ways.[57] These "higher" thoughts and ways have been revealed in the Bible.[58] Repentance is turning from one's own sinful thoughts and ways to biblical truth and holiness.[59]

Confession is inseparably linked with repentance. It is the outward expression to others of the inner admission to oneself that one was wrong in thought, word, attitude, or behavior. It is a verbal admission of wrongdoing made in the presence of the wronged party. The word *confess* means literally, "to say the same thing." It is, therefore, verbal agreement to the scriptural evaluation of his behavior as sin.[60]

Restitution

The important biblical concept of restitution should also be considered. When a person has injured someone else, God says that he "must confess the sin he has committed . . . [and] make full restitution for his wrong."[61] In the New Testament, this is what Zacchaeus did when he was led to repentance by the Lord Jesus. Zacchaeus did not merely ask for forgiveness and go on about his business. Instead, he stood up in front of Jesus and the people he had wronged and said, "Look, Lord! Here and now I give half of my possessions to the poor, and if I have cheated anybody out of anything, I will pay back four times the amount."[62]

Restitution produces several benefits. According to Sande, "As much as possible, it restores the injured party to his or her former position. Restitution also benefits society by making destructive behavior unprofitable. In addition, it gives the offender an opportunity to make amends for sin and to demonstrate by actions that he or she wishes to be restored to the injured person and to society in general."[63] It serves to ingrain lessons that will help the offender avoid similar wrongdoing in the future.[64]

Restitution can be an integral part of the process of forgiveness and reconciliation. Being forgiven by the injured party does not necessarily release the offender from responsibility to repair the damage. An injured party may exercise mercy, and in some cases it is good to waive the right to restitution.[65] However; in many cases, making restitution is beneficial even for the offender. Doing so demonstrates remorse, sincerity, and a new attitude, which can help speed reconciliation. [66]

CHAPTER EIGHT

RECONCILIATION IN RELATIONSHIPS

In the previous chapter, forgiveness as a matter of the heart was discussed. Conflict starts in the heart.[1] The book of James says: "What causes fights and quarrels among you? Don't they come from your desires that battle within you? You want something but don't get it. You kill and covet, but you cannot have what you want. You quarrel and fight. You do not have, because you do not ask God. When you ask, you do not receive, because you ask with wrong motives, that you may spend what you get on your pleasures."[2]

Conflict and Reconciliation in Relationships

In the gospel of Mark, Jesus says: "What comes out of a man is what makes him 'unclean.' For from within, out of men's hearts, come evil thoughts, sexual immorality, theft, murder, adultery, greed, malice, deceit, lewdness, envy, slander, arrogance and folly. All these evils come from inside and make a man 'unclean.'"[3] Our hearts are the wellsprings of all our thoughts, desires, words, and actions. Therefore, it is also the source of our conflicts.[4] These passages describe the root cause of conflict, which is unmet desires in our hearts. When we want something and feel that we will not be satisfied unless we get it, that desire starts to control us. If others fail to meet our desires, we sometimes condemn them in our hearts and fight harder to get our own way. Sande says it this way:

> James 4:1-3 provides a key principle for understanding and resolving conflict.
>
> Whenever we have a serious dispute with others, we should always look carefully at our own hearts to see whether we are being controlled by unmet desires that we have turned into idols. These desires love to disguise themselves as things we need or deserve, or even as things that would advance God's kingdom. But no matter how good or legitimate a desire may look on the surface, if we have gotten to the point where we cannot be content, fulfilled, or secure unless we have it, that desire has evolved into an idol that has diverted our love and trust from God. Fortunately, God delights to deliver us from our slavery to idols and enable us to find true freedom, fulfillment, and security in his love and provision.[5]

In order for people to break free from ungodly desires that spring from within and condemning judgments which fuel conflict with others, the practice of forgiveness and reconciliation must be engaged. This practice is an essential ingredient for living a godly and productive life and glorifying God. It is a skill that affects who people are and how they relate to others in their world.[6] To the degree to which it is practiced diligently, it allows persons to develop mastery over wounding and live in harmony with others in the world.

Family Relationships

The twentieth century western mind sees man very individualistically, as if we can look at one man at a time. American society at large considers individualism and self-sufficiency as noble characteristics of a person. This is not the way God sees mankind. God sees man in terms of families, and He thinks in terms of generations.[7] Scripture often says, "I am the God of Abraham, Isaac, and Jacob."[8]

At times, God speaks of several hundred years as if it were an extremely short time. Consider His promise to give Abraham the land of Canaan. Over 400 years passed between the time of the promise and the realization of the promise. From the foundation of the world, God planned every individual. In His mind, we already existed before we were born.[9] Hebrews portrays Levi as having already tithed because he existed in Abraham's loins when Abraham tithed.[10]

As discussed earlier, since the Fall in the Garden, people are born under the curse of sin.[11] Parents often repeat the sins of their fathers (and mothers). They may replicate sinful attitudes, prejudices, values and/or conflicts, which their children assimilate from their parents. In addition, the parents' sin usually has hurtful consequences in the lives of the offspring, causing them to form misconceptions of God and wrong thinking based on their hurts.[12] Hence, besides being an interpersonal matter, forgiveness and reconciliation must sometimes be observed as an interfamilial matter.

Intergenerational Patterns

The misdeeds of one generation often put pressure on the next generation to enter into those same misdeeds and sins.[13] The sins are continued with the usual consequence of the hurts being inflicted on others as well as on the person who is sinning. For example, an alcoholic, especially if he is married and has children, usually inflicts a great number of hurts on the immediate family, extended family, friends, and business associates. The resulting curses usually involve some form of alienation, destruction, or death that causes major hurts to all involved.[14]

Sometimes when the sins and curses coming down a family line are more pronounced like alcoholism, drug use, or sexual abuse, the problem is easily identified. The root cause and how to eradicate it from the family line, however, are not so easy. With "less serious" sins, the source of the problem is sometimes not even identified as generational. People tend to underestimate the significance of generational transmission of sins and conflicts.

Scripture says, "You shall not make for yourself an idol in the form of anything in heaven above or on the earth beneath or in the waters below. You shall not bow down to them or worship them; for I, the Lord your God, am a jealous God, punishing the children for the sin of the fathers to the third and fourth generation of those who hate me, but showing love to a thousand [generations] of those who love me and keep my commandments."[15]

"Sin of the fathers" represents the accumulation of all sins committed by and learned from our ancestors. It is the heart tendency (iniquity) that we inherit from our forefathers to rebel (i.e. be disobedient) against God's laws and commandments.[16] It is the influence and propensity to sin, particularly in ways that represent perversion and twisted character.[17] Unholy generational patterns may sometimes manifest as idolatry.[18]

Idol worship can be very subtle. "Idolatry occurs whenever we put our trust in the 'thing' or 'situation' more than we put our trust in God."[19] It occurs as a person looks for information, power, fulfillment, and satisfaction in things apart from God. Idolatry's misplaced passions and desires often create unrealistic demands on others that create offense and conflict in relationships. God created mankind for love, companionship, and fellowship. After the Fall, iniquity became the inner tendency of man's heart to rebel against God's created design and exercise self to be in control of his destiny.[20]

Every person is responsible for his own sin. However, sometimes the Bible talks about a corporate aspect to sin and corporate repentance to be practiced as well.[21] Leviticus says, "But if they will confess their sins and the sins of their fathers—their treachery against me and their hostility toward me, ... then when their uncircumcised hearts are humbled and they pay for their sin, I will remember my covenant with Jacob and my covenant with Isaac and my covenant with Abraham, and I will remember the land."[22] Some practice a principle called "identificational repentance" whereby people identify with their ancestors and repent on their behalf as well as their own.[23] They believe this breaks the power of the propensity to sin in a specific manner. Examples of this principle in Scripture are found in Daniel 9, Ezra 9, and Nehemiah 2 and 9. It must be noted that although certain sins may be familiar to a generational line because of innate sin, each person must repent and ask forgiveness for his own sin before God. More corporate aspects of forgiveness and reconciliation will be discussed in later sections.

Marriage Relationships

The marriage relationship is central to the family unit. When a marital union commences, two intergenerational families combine into one. The interpersonal relationship of the married couple is living out the combined effects of all the previous generations' relationships. Hence the spousal relationship provides a unique opportunity to practice forgiveness and reconciliation.[24] The physical act of "leaving and cleaving" presents some spiritual challenges in living as one.[25]

Ephesians chapter five describes the biblical pattern for a husband and wife relationship. "A man will leave his father and mother and be united to his wife, and the two will become one flesh."[26] The marriage relationship is designed by God to provide unique opportunities for two persons to demonstrate love and commitment. "Husbands, love your wives, just as Christ loved the church and gave himself up for her."[27] The biblical view of love within marriage includes a commitment so deep it is presented as a type of Christ's love for his Bride. Christ's example of love and forgiveness discussed earlier is particularly significant for the marital covenant. The Bible clearly shows that Christ's love and commitment to reconciliation is to be exemplified in the marriage relationship.

Couples who nurture their relationship by practicing forgiveness and reconciliation have a much better chance of seeing the fruit of forgiveness in their children's lives. As the primary caretakers in their children's lives, parents have the primary responsibility of training children to love and forgive.[28] Flowing from the marriage relationship, God designed the family unit to influence the ability of the next generation to receive God's love and forgiveness and give it to others.

Church Relationships

God not only designed the process of forgiveness and reconciliation for individual and family relationships to be the best they can be, but God's purposes are much larger. God is building a family of His very own—a kingdom of sons and daughters. He restores relationships to be an expression of unity for Kingdom purposes.[29]

The first sin fractured unity. It broke the unity between mankind and heaven. It fractured the unity between man and woman. It destroyed the unity between man and nature.[30] God wants us to share in the restoration of unity throughout creation, fulfilling His purpose throughout the heavens and the earth. Through the Church, He wants to bring all creation into His eternal purpose.[31] Forgiveness is the seat of unity for the restoration of the Kingdom of God. "How good and pleasant it is when brothers live together in unity! It is like precious oil … It is as if the dew of Hermon were falling on Mount Zion. For there the Lord bestows his blessing, even life forevermore."[32]

The level of unity discernable among members of a church congregation is indicative of the overall health of that body of believers. If there is disunity, there will be heaviness, rancor, and distrust. If there is unity, there is lightness, joy, and a sense of blessing pouring over all. Forgiveness restores unity, and only where unity exists can blessing be poured out.[33]

The Church is riddled with the effects of unforgiveness. Unforgiveness distorts truth and locks people in their own subjective perceptions of reality.[34] Discernment becomes warped because issues are interpreted from a childish, ungodly point of view.[35] Unforgiveness causes people to fall short of the grace of God.[36] It causes stress from unresolved debt and cycles of sin.[37] It destroys any hope for resolving conflict by taking away the ability to lovingly confront others and to receive correction from others.[38] The disunity caused by unforgiveness makes the Church more vulnerable to attacks by Satan.[39] It creates facades; superficiality; distrust; and lack of transparency, honesty and integrity.[40] It creates exhaustion![41]

The heart of Jesus is for His Bride, the Church. "The Spirit and the bride say, 'Come!' And let him who hears say, 'Come!' Whoever is thirsty, let him come; and whoever wishes, let him take the free gift of the water of life."[42] Forgiveness is the "free gift of the water of life." Christ's forgiveness is transforming the Church into a beautiful Bride.

Forgiveness changes hardness of heart into compassion. People become consistently pure and transparent. Forgiveness makes life richer, more filled with love, more expansive, more spiritually alive, more abundantly satisfying. Although people may disagree with others, they appreciate the differences. They begin to value diversity. They learn to appreciate people for the way they provide balance for the whole—lifting, enriching, blessing, fulfilling, challenging and sometimes wounding as well. Forgiving helps make people appreciate the ways differences, challenges, rebukes, and wounds drive them to perfection for Him. People walking in forgiveness also provide the means by which God's Kingdom is established on earth and the Father's blessing is extended.[43]

Spiritual authority is granted through forgiveness. "Again Jesus said, "Peace be with you! As the Father has sent me, I am sending you." And with that he breathed on them and said, "Receive the Holy Spirit. If you forgive anyone his sins, they are forgiven; if you do not forgive them, they are not forgiven."[44] God's authority is carried out through his people receiving and granting forgiveness.

Peace and rest are also granted through forgiveness. "Come to me, all you who are weary and burdened, and I will give you rest. Take my yoke upon you and learn from me, for I am gentle and humble in heart, and you will find rest for your souls."[45] Forgiveness provides a framework for authenticity in relationships. It relieves the stress of trying to hide the inconsistencies in one's life. Forgiveness and reconciliation reveal a heart of trust in God's plan for repentance and rest as the means of salvation.[46]

Community Relationships

These same principles apply similarly to relationships outside the Body of Christ. Demanding one's rights when faced with another's actions that disappoint or offend will usually make the person defensive and hesitant to admit one's wrong. Conflict is generally made worse by pointing out what people have done wrong and what should be done to make it right.[47]

Sande says in *Peacemaking for Families*, "The Lord is graciously working to teach me a better way to approach others about their failures. Instead of coming at them with the law, I am learning to bring them the gospel. In other words, rather than dwelling on what people should do or have failed to do I am learning to focus primarily on what God has done and is doing for them through Christ."[48] This approach is demonstrated and commended throughout Scripture. Consider Jesus' conversation with the Samaritan woman. Instead of hammering away at her sinful lifestyle, Jesus spent most of his time engaging her in a conversation about salvation, eternal life, true worship, and the coming of the Messiah.[49] She responded eagerly to this gospel-focused approach, let down her defenses, and put her trust in Christ. Although Jesus changed this focus when rebuking hard-hearted Pharisees, his typical approach to bringing people to repentance was to bring them the good news of God's forgiveness.[50]

Sande also provides a valuable exhortation:

> Although it is often best simply to overlook the sins of others there will be times when doing so only prolongs alienation and encourages them to continue acting in a hurtful manner. If you know that someone has something against you, go to that person and talk about it as soon as possible. Similarly, if someone's sins are dishonoring God, damaging your relationship, hurting others, or hurting that person, one of the most loving and helpful things you can do is go and help him or her see the need for change. With God's grace and the right words (including your own confession), such a

conversation will often lead to restored peace
and stronger relationships.[51]

The familiar Scripture text of Matthew 18 gives the biblical exhortation and methodology for restoring broken relationships. It protects both the offender and the person offended. "If your brother sins against you, go and show him his fault, just between the two of you. If he listens to you, you have won your brother over. But if he will not listen, take one or two others along, so that 'every Matt may be established by the testimony of two or three witnesses.' If he refuses to listen to them, tell it to the church; and if he refuses to listen even to the church, treat him as you would a pagan or a tax collector."[52] After this Peter asked Jesus how many times he should forgive his brother, to which Jesus answered, "I tell you, not seven times, but seventy-seven times." Then Jesus shared the parable of the unmerciful servant (described previously) in which he drives home the point that God initiated a way to become free of debtors› prison. Here Jesus describes forgiveness as the centerpiece of the "kingdom of heaven."[53]

Personal Forgiveness in Context of Community

As a person matures in his knowledge of the importance of practicing forgiveness and reconciliation, he will understand the value of confession and repentance in facilitating open (transparent) relationships. As a general rule, an offender should confess his sins to each person who has been directly affected by his wrongdoing. Since all sins offend God by violating His will, all sins should be first confessed to Him.[54] Whether a sin should be confessed to other people as well as to God depends on whether it was a "heart sin" or a "social sin."[55] A heart sin takes place only in the thoughts and does not directly affect others. Therefore, it needs to be confessed only to God. A social sin involves words or actions that actually affect other people. This may include acts of commission, such as slandering, stealing, or lying, or acts of omission, such as failing to help someone in need or ignoring someone. Social sins should be confessed to those who have been affected by them, whether it is a single individual or a group of people who were affected by, or even witnessed, the action(s).[56] In general, a person's confession should reach as far as the offense.[57]

For a person at the victim end of a "sin of omission," it may be a particularly difficult journey through forgiveness and reconciliation. In the previous Part Two, two major areas of releasing were discussed: God and other persons. In the context of community, another area of yielding emerges—an institution. What happens when organizations in society (government, education, business, human service) offend intentionally or unintentionally? They may inflict deep perceived wounds on unsuspecting people. Examples may be corporations cutting back their work force by eliminating jobs indiscriminately, social service agencies unfairly neglecting individuals with the most need, or the justice system following the legal rule book to drag innocent by-standers (including children) through gross details of violence and crime.

Some say institutions cannot be forgiven. Smedes says only people can be forgiven, and therefore suggests finding a responsible person in the organization to forgive[58] and work through the process of reconciliation. While this may be helpful in some cases, more often than not, this is not possible. As discussed earlier, forgiveness is surrendering the debt of an offender to be paid by the blood of God's Son Jesus Christ. Whoever, or whatever, created the debt must be surrendered to God in order to receive grace and mercy from the God who is able to pay it. A Christian's willingness to release bitterness and resentment, even without the remotest possibility of blame being attached, is in a position to receive God's grace of forgiveness and give it as others need it.[59]

Intercultural Forgiveness

Another deeply challenging area of forgiveness and reconciliation is in intercultural relationships. Many people avoid entering into these relationships completely, but God's heart is for people of all tribes and tongues, not just uniformly existing together, but unified in accomplishing His purposes on earth.[60]

In this very brief discussion of the topic, first a definition is in order. Craig Storti, in his book *Figuring Foreigners Out* defines *culture* this way: "Culture is the shared assumptions, values, and beliefs of a group of people which result in characteristic behaviors."[61] The things people believe and value are based on assumptions developed over time and influenced by other people living in proximity. Behavior is a direct result of what people assume, value, or believe in.[62]

As discussed earlier, honesty and humility are key ingredients in the process of forgiveness. The lack of honesty and humility in people's personal lives, translates into lack of ability to be vulnerable and transparent in community life. Acknowledgement and ownership of values and beliefs makes the way for genuine communication to occur. On both ends of sending and receiving a message, values and beliefs impact interpretation of verbal and nonverbal interactions. Since communication is the most essential action in preventing and resolving offense,[63] it becomes imperative to discover unknown assumptions which may be driving reactions and responses to others' behaviors. Differences in perceptions (sometimes unknown) create filters toward biases and preferences.

Cultural Diversity

In the letter to the Ephesians Paul shows that unity does not mean uniformity of values and beliefs.[64] He reminds the reader that God has richly blessed his children with a wide array of gifts, talents, and callings.[65] Mature Christians rejoice in the diversity that God has given to his people, and they realize that believers can legitimately hold differences of opinion on "disputable matters."[66] When differences rob us of harmony and peace with God and man, however, there is work to do in realms of forgiveness and reconciliation.[67]

Later in Ephesians, Paul uses even stronger language to emphasize the importance of harmonious relationships. He warns his readers that they "grieve the Holy Spirit" when they indulge in unwholesome talk . . . bitterness, rage and anger, brawling and slander."[68] Knowing that such conduct grieves God and quenches the work of the Holy Spirit in peoples' lives, Paul earnestly urges readers to "be kind and compassionate to one another, forgiving each other, just as in Christ God forgave you."[69]

In fact, the Bible teaches that some differences are natural and beneficial. Since God creates us as unique individuals, human beings will often have different opinions, convictions, desires, perspectives, and priorities. Many of these differences are not inherently right or wrong; they are simply the result of God-given diversity and personal preferences.[70] When handled properly, disagreements in these areas can stimulate productive dialogue, encourage creativity, promote helpful change, and generally make life more interesting.[71] Therefore, although people should seek unity in their relationships, they should not demand uniformity.[72] Instead of avoiding all conflicts or demanding that others always agree, they should rejoice in the diversity of God's creation and learn to accept and work with people who simply see things differently than they do.[73]

Cultural Unforgiveness

Christians are not only called to practice cultural diversity in their relations with other believers, but also in society at large.[74] This has taken on a somewhat different outlook within the last half century with a change in how groups (cultures and subcultures) are perceived and identified. Historically, groups have operated on the basis of a majority rule, with some respect for minority opinion. In more recent times, postmodernism and multiculturalism have valued the identity of almost every group that perceives itself as being socially unique.[75] The group is considered to have rights and has demanded those rights. This has created a more contentious atmosphere. The contention is increasing.

Because issues of justice and inequity have become more salient, people in different groups have increasingly re-examined the past and discovered instances of discrimination, prejudice, and failure to receive their perceived just rights. This has led such groups to construct an argument that emphasizes a need to obtain more of society's resources and respect from other groups. Perceptions of inequality have generated feelings of unforgiveness in many of the group members. Groups contain people who take offense and sometimes try to steer the group in a direction that ultimately hurts their cause.[76]

Inter-group tensions are inevitable, but they sometimes erupt into group conflicts. People are social beings and array themselves into groups. In fact, all persons belong to countless groups in categories of political, religious, and socioeconomic groups containing persons who hold various attitudes about government structures, eating meat, owning property, etc. When people interact with group members and those who threaten their group boundary, psychological processes are set in motion that powerfully influence behavior and the behavior of one group against another group.[77] Although beyond the scope of this project, an interesting question arises: how does one promote forgiveness and reconciliation among people whose lives are intimately intertwined with each other, or who may have a history of conflict and transgressions against each other that might stretch back for centuries? The Christian view holds the greatest hope for societal forgiveness and reconciliation.

Gender, Race, Ethnicity and Religion

The most common societal differences that create divisions needing reconciliation focus around areas of gender, race, ethnicity, and religion. Often centered on the topic of marriage relationships, many books are written to highlight the differences in male and female thinking and behavior patterns. Some say that efforts to emphasize "equal rights for women" have led to an unhealthy blending of the genders, confusing roles and disregarding differences built into the genders by the Creator Himself (Baars 2003, 129). No doubt, differences exist between men and women. However, men differ from other men, and women differ from other women more than the average man differs from the average woman.[78]

Similar to gender, the central issues of race relations revolve around equality, which is seen to differ within the races and ethnicity. In the United States, the conflict has traditionally been between whites and blacks, but recent demographics have shown an increase in numbers of Asian and Hispanic minorities. Power struggles are at the root of racial conflict.[79] Historically, the practice of slavery (in the United States) has had an obvious impact on the ability of the white and black race to reconcile differences.

Groups centered on religious beliefs can also become embroiled in a power struggle. As an example of religious tensions, the politics of the 1960s and 1970s embraced a strong doctrine of separation of religion and state. As this doctrine became more widespread, people who were highly religious, especially those conservative in their religion, began to resent that their most important values were not allowed to figure into state policies. Thus, people with strongly held theologically conservative beliefs and values began to bring those values into political decision-making. So-called conservative principles, such as the sanctity of human life, were applied with religious force in some areas, such as abortion and euthanasia. Conservative religious people became more politically active and better organized and have had more political effect in the last fifteen years than have religious moderates or liberals.[80] This built resistance and, in some cases, has divided religious groups along political lines. Throughout the centuries, many examples could be cited where hostilities have arisen from irreconcilable differences in belief systems.

Minority Status

People's similarities attract them to groups based on likeness. People tend to avoid those with whom they lack similarity.[81] Social conventions, jobs, and other societal structures thrust people into interactions with members of groups with whom they find themselves dissimilar to, not attracted to, and in competition with. Perception hardens the group boundaries. The more individuals think about being a member of a group, concentrate on the differences and competition, and note the affect associated with the members of the two groups, the more people tend to see the world in terms of those two groups.[82] As a consequence, people identify more or less strongly with one of those two groups. Group identity and the strength of that identity end up being an important aspect of when and how hurts can be healed, memories amended, and relationships reconciled. The more minority group members feel taken advantage of by members of a more privileged group, the more difficult reconciliation becomes.

Conflict is inevitable in relationships and among groups.[83] Realizing that conflict is almost inevitable does not mean that people should retreat from it or abandon who they are and what they believe in. Christians especially should work to minimize divisive conflict in order to maintain peaceful conditions as long as they possibly can for reasons heretofore mentioned. In addition, the hope is to establish restored relationship from past conflicts and set up just social conditions that will make future conflicts less likely.[84]

Historically Speaking

Through the ages, many examples could be cited where major conflict and disastrous consequences emerged from people refusing to reconcile their differences and extend forgiveness to fellowman. Several centuries ago, instrumental in the founding of the United States, a man named William Penn had vision for peace and reconciliation as part of something he called the "Holy Experiment." Darrell Fields, in a book called *The Seed of a Nation*, details Penn's heart for the fair treatment of the "first nation" (native Indian) people. After Penn's death, the actions of his sons reversed Penn's efforts. Subsequent generations entered into a dark period in the history of the European settlement of "Penn's Woods" (Pennsylvania) and surrounding regions. The native people were tricked and squeezed out of their land. Seeds of discord, bitterness, and resentment were sown, the fruit of which Americans still reap to this day.[85]

Centuries have come and gone since Penn's ideals were drafted into the founding documents of what became the government of the United States of America. Although the "Holy Experiment" attracted many religious people to the "melting pot" of ethnicities, no earthly government can substitute for the Kingdom of God working forgiveness and reconciliation in the heart of its people.[86]

In the heart of Pennsylvania lies an Amish community that recently endured a serious test of its commitment to forgiveness and reconciliation. On October 2, 2006, the innocence of the Amish West Nickel Mines schoolhouse was intruded by a non-Amish neighbor-gunman who shot ten female students before turning the gun on himself. As the story unfolded in the news media, along with the usual Amish themes of simplicity of lifestyle and nonviolent response to aggression, the major topic became "forgiveness." How could the Amish forgive the gunman so quickly and resolutely and extend acts of kindness to his family members left behind?

Since the shooting in 2006, several books have been written on the subject of the Amish and their history of forgiveness as a people. One book, entitled *Amish Grace,* records many accounts of the authors' interviews with Amish individuals:

> A father who lost a daughter at the schoolhouse stressed again and again that forgiveness is more than words. Sitting at his kitchen table, he told us, "Our forgiveness is not in our words, it's in our actions; it's not what we said, but what we did. That was our forgiveness." At the bottom of his faxed correspondence, another Amish man included a phrase that he had borrowed from a church sign: 'Preach the gospel, and if necessary, use words.' The Amish were preaching, but rarely with words.[87]

Though too deep a topic to adequately cover here, the culture and theology of forgiveness in the Amish community have historical roots which are perhaps unparalleled in the entire world. The Amish of Lancaster County, Pennsylvania, descend from the *Anabaptists,* a radical Christian movement that arose in Europe in 1525, shortly after Martin Luther launched the Protestant Reformation. Opponents of the young radicals called them *Anabaptists,* a derogatory nickname meaning "rebaptizers," because they baptized one another as adults even though they had been baptized as infants in the state church. These radical reformers sought to create Christian communities marked by love for each other and love for their enemies, an ethic they based on the life and teaching of Jesus. Anabaptists would not use violence, nor would they ask government officials to coerce or otherwise maintain religious belief. They believed that the faithful church should not rely on state support or sanction whatsoever. For them, any links to the state were a sure sign that the church had compromised its primary commitment to God.[88]

Such ideas earned Anabaptists the ire of both Catholic and Protestant church leaders, who perceived their authority to be undercut, and civic officials, who relied on religious fear to keep citizens in line. Condemned on all sides, Anabaptists soon found themselves imprisoned and even executed for their beliefs. Although the Anabaptist movement was never large, it accounted for 40 to 50 percent of all Western European Christians who were martyred for their faith during the sixteenth century. Although martyrs are a minority in any movement, and most Anabaptists never faced the prospect of capital punishment, nevertheless, brutal death has been a part of the Anabaptists' story from the time they began creating their cultural uniqueness.[89]

The five girls who lost their lives at the schoolhouse joined the sixteenth-century martyrs of the Amish faith. The old martyr stories are recorded in a thousand-page book, *The Bloody Theater or Martyrs Mirror of the Defenseless Christians,* known simply as *Martyrs Mirror.*[90] Amish ministers often cite this massive tome in their sermons.

The book *Amish Grace* records, "in the minds of many Amish people, they [the five girls] were martyrs. 'They were willing to die, and that makes them martyrs,' said one Amish mother. The oldest one said, 'Shoot me first'."[91] Perhaps it was the stories of the martyrs in her people's history that imbued the oldest girl with such courage on that terrifying day. The stories and songs of the faith that she had learned will certainly be passed down to generations after hers. Her response certainly passed the ultimate test of self-denial.

People's actions are rarely random. Individuals embrace patterns of behavior and habits of mind and heart that shape what they do in a given situation. The collective behavior or patterns of a group is considered *culture.*[92] Culture can be compared to a musical repertoire. A repertoire is a set of musical pieces that a performer knows especially well from frequent practice. It reflects an artist's background and training, and serves a performer in a situation in which there is no time to learn something new. When musicians or a choral group is asked to perform on short notice, they must fall back on their repertoire—the material they can perform almost instinctively. It's not that musicians can't learn new music; they often do. Even then, however, a repertoire forms the core around which new material is added.

Culture is the term we use for a group's repertoire of beliefs and behaviors. It involves assumptions and conduct that are so deeply rooted and so often practiced that most people are not even aware of them. Culture reflects people's history and teaching and is especially visible in times of stress that demand immediate response, when there is no time or emotional energy to think through all the possible actions. Like musical repertoires, cultures change over time, but they change in ways that extend present patterns.

As mentioned earlier, focusing on God is the key to resolving conflict through forgiveness and reconciliation. Remembering His mercy and drawing on His strength help people see things more clearly and respond more wisely. This also is the way Christians can show others that there really is a God and that He delights in helping those who yield to His grace. In his Word, God explains how bitterness and resentment develop and how they should be dealt with. If only people could respond more like Christ Jesus.

Author, historian, and Mennonite pastor of fifty-seven years, John Ruth, in his book simply called *Forgiveness,* affirms the universality of Christ-centered forgiveness and reconciliation as the best way to achieve genuine transformation in the world. He writes:

> Around the time of the attack at Nickel Mines an international group of scholars studying at the University of Pennsylvania visited our congregation, thirty miles north of Philadelphia. They were taken to the nearby Mennonite Heritage Center, with its then current exhibit on the themes of peace, forgiveness, and reconciliation. Statements from Scripture, Menno Simons, Elie Wiesel, Nelson Mandela,

the father of a man beheaded in Iraq, a Mennonite nurse, and others were placed in a kind of timeline. One of the South African visitors seemed especially struck by the exhibit. Her husband, she revealed, had been murdered in the troubles of recent decades. This had left her terminally angry, hating the persons who had caused her pain. But something happened to her as she moved across the exhibit, carefully reading statement after statement of forgiveness and calls for reconciliation. Overwhelmed by the cumulative effect, she flatly informed her fellow students, "I'm not the same person as the one who came in here. When I go back to South Africa, my friends will not know me. I have made the decision to forgive."[93]

The Christian world view is about changing a heart of bitterness and rebellion, primarily against God and secondarily against fellowman, into a heart of Christ-like forgiving grace. It's about changing a heart of stone into a heart of flesh, [94] so the world can see the Word made flesh.[95] Forgiveness and reconciliation beg to be the core of a Christian's life song repertoire.

CHAPTER NINE

CONCLUSION

This book began by exploring the tremendous gap between what Christians believe and what they practice concerning forgiveness. Although many think they understand and practice forgiveness, the high incidence of health problems and the great amount of unresolved relational conflict show otherwise. Misunderstandings of forgiveness occur when merely focusing on outward symptoms rather than examining heart issues of ungodly judgments, roots of bitterness, and resentment. Christians must also turn their attention to the nature and character of their Creator, in whose image and likeness they were created.

We also examined what the Bible has to say and some recent research on the topic of forgiveness. The four key statements below guided the discussion centered on four themes. The first is the redemptive plan of God; second, the centrality of Jesus Christ; third, practicing the elements of forgiveness; and four, paving the way for reconciliation and conflict resolution.

1. *The Christian understanding of forgiveness must be contextualized in the purposes of God's redemptive history.*

God created man to be a living soul[1] in His very image.[2] Many of the modern psychological works on forgiveness merely capture the soul dynamics of the created self, but fail to capture comprehensively the dynamics associated with the fallen and redeemed self with respect to the supernatural realm of good and evil. God's love does its perfecting work in the human soul,[3] battling the strongholds opposed to the truths of God and "taking every thought captive to the obedience of Christ."[4] Renewing of the mind includes the change of negative thinking patterns, core beliefs, emotions associated with the fruit of forgiveness,[5] and attitudes and actions, since love does not rejoice in unrighteousness.[6]

Most important in man's collaboration with God's perfecting work is an increasing awareness of and distaste for one's own sin. The awareness of sin's effect upon oneself in the moral and natural realms brings about increased humility.[7] Moreover, the putting off of the old fleshly self and the putting on of the new spiritual self is a continual dynamic (process) that characterizes the sanctifying work of God's love in the redeemed soul.[8] As God's love continues to purify the heart, there is an increasing disposition to actions and attitudes that are congruent with loving one's neighbor and even one's enemy. The efficacious work of divine love in the soul yields forgiveness and the fruit of the Spirit.[9] Allowing God to change the soul to forgive like Christ is a work of pursuing holiness. Ultimately, forgiveness is the consummate expression of Christ-likeness.[10]

2. *A biblical understanding of forgiveness must be centered on the foundational framework of the life, death, and resurrection of Jesus Christ.*

For a Christian to experience "true" (complete) forgiveness, it must be forgiveness that Christ accomplishes through faith in the finished work of His death on the Cross and resurrection. By practicing a type of "forgiveness" attempted outside of Christ, a measure of healthy living may be attained; however, life in Christ yields experiences of forgiveness in the fullest extent possible. Forgiving an offender his offense may release some emotional resentment and bitterness and may even allow positive emotional movement towards the offender. Only Christ, however, can fully resolve the depth of indebtedness that is required for the fullest extent of the surrender effecting perfect justice and mercy at the same time. Forgiveness without Christ can become little more than "dead works." Since the Bible teaches that Christ has accomplished forgiveness,[11] claiming to arrive at forgiveness without the work of Christ at the center of this experience, can become, in essence, a rejection of his free gift of grace, and a means of self-glorification.[12]

3. *The four elements to be applied in practicing forgiveness are:*

☐ Receive the gift of forgiveness Christ has already foregiven,

☐ Yield to God in forgiving (releasing) the offender and surrender the offense to His judgment,

☐ Redirect energy from blaming the other person to believing God's ability to change the heart, and

☐ Practice these steps as often as is needed for all offenses on life's journey.

Forgiveness flows from the redeemed soul as God's love does its perfecting work. Genuine transformation takes place when one is compelled to forgive, not out of mere moral obligation, but out of one's love for God and concern for the spiritual condition of the other's soul. Even love for an enemy flows from a pure heart, out of joy, gratitude, and a love for righteousness, initiated not by any conditional responses on the part of the offender, but initiated by the love of God and for the love for God. Regarding the volitional aspect of forgiveness, forgiveness involves submitting to the will of God[13] for the sake of one's relationship with God. As one travels the path of forgiveness seventy times seven, the offering of redemptive love for the spiritual welfare of others becomes increasingly a way of life,[14] rather than a distinct act or methodological framework. The more forgiveness is practiced, the more it becomes woven into the journey of life.

Yielding to God is necessary in releasing an offender from his offense. Honesty and humility are key components in acknowledging one's need to forgive. In order to practice true forgiveness, both believing and discerning components must be involved in journeying completely through the sanctification process. Confession, repentance, blessing, and restitution are key ingredients in the process. They demonstrate the fruit of an honest assessment and humble heart. The offended person's willingness to take responsibility for any part he or she plays in causing the offense demonstrates a true heart of humility, shows the love of God, and opens the door for reconciliation in the proper timing.

When people pray and unconditionally forgive, they are turning over to God the penalty of the offense for His judgment, His justice, His punishment, or whatever He determines to do about it. For the purpose of deciding whether or not to release to God the penalty of the offense, it matters not whether the supposed offender is really guilty. God knows. Supposed victims do not always know. A person's responsibility is to pray, trust God, and turn it over to God to judge.[15]

Forgiving an offender produces the fruit of good health in body, mind, and spirit.[16] Many physical illnesses can be attributed to an unhealthy spiritual condition. Besides blaming an offender, sometimes blaming God, or blaming oneself can create sinful and unhealthy burdens that need to be released to come into wholeness of body, mind, and spirit. The sanctifying (healing) journey for each person is unique and may lead one through varying degrees of adversity. Struggles or even suffering should not be minimized, feared, or avoided because God causes all things to work together for good.[17]

4. *Forgiveness and reconciliation are inevitable experiences in worthwhile interpersonal relationships, stirred by conflict and testing of character in a broken world that is not repairable (humanly speaking).*

Perhaps the most radical attribute of God-centered love and forgiveness is self-denial. In God's divine wisdom, the way of ensuring the best for oneself is to deny oneself,[18] trusting in the faithfulness and loving kindness of God.[19] The losing of self to gain an abundant life in Christ is the greatest paradox of human existence and is thoroughly God-centered. When questioned about the greatest commandment, Jesus answered: "'Love the Lord your God with all your heart and with all your soul and with all your strength and with all your mind'; and, 'Love your neighbor as yourself'" (Luke 10:27).

God's two-fold commandment to love confronts and challenges the human tendency for selfish, preferential love. To give oneself for the sake of another through forgiving love follows the supreme example of Christ and fulfills God's purpose in suffering—to know Christ more intimately.[20]

The other-centeredness of divine love and forgiveness joins individuals with God and one another and serves as the driving force that leads to restoration and reconciliation.[21] Love for a neighbor and love for an enemy exist only when shared and work as the bond to create and strengthen community, while embodying God's relational paradigm for the coming kingdom of heaven.[22]

Every aspect of forgiveness is focused on God and His love. One of the purposes of forgiveness is that both the offended and offender might love God more deeply, which is congruent with life lived out in redemptive history. Therefore, forgiveness is redemptive. Forgiveness not only sanctifies the forgiver, but can also be used by God to redeem and sanctify the forgiven; accordingly, forgiveness is instrumental in expanding and edifying the body of Christ.[23]

The Church, as a diverse family of God's people and as a community centered in God's love, must learn to allow cultural and theological differences to unite rather than divide. Christians should rejoice in the diversity God has given to His people, [24] and should welcome believers' legitimate differences of opinion on "disputable matters."[25] Individuals in the Body of Christ need to practice forgiveness and reconciliation, not only for themselves (to fulfill God's sanctifying purposes), but also to become a community engaged in God's mission of reconciling the world to Himself.[26]

Becoming Free through Forgiveness

Forgiveness involves three main components: the Gift, the choice, and the fruit (i.e. Jesus as God's Gift of love, our choice to surrender, and the human experience that follows). Arguments in scholarly writing as to defining what forgiveness is or is not, center on degrees of involvement of these three elements. God the Father gave the Gift of His Son Jesus Christ, so that whosoever believes (chooses to receive the Gift) has his sins forgiven, and receives the Holy Spirit sent by Jesus to continue His work in people's lives[27] and demonstrate the fruit. Forgiveness is the gift of God, received by man with mind and heart, to be given as "life" to others. After the Fall (creating the debt unable to be paid), Jesus came to save the broken world,[28] accomplishing the work of forgiveness. Jesus then turned appropriation of forgiveness over to the Holy Spirit,[29] who is actively convicting and guiding people's hearts toward forgiveness. Forgiveness cannot be accomplished by people's choice to forgive alone, but it is the power of the Holy Spirit that gives people the grace to receive the Gift, model the Gift, and teach it to the world.[30] It is truly a work of God to forgive and be forgiven and to be reconciled to God and with man.

Mental health treatment, for persons professing to be disciples of Jesus Christ, must revolve around a God-centered approach to the topic of forgiveness and reconciliation. To be walking in the fullness of a life of discipleship, a person must first have an accurate understanding of God's redemptive plan in history. From a position of humility, a person must then be honest about his own personal condition before God and be willing to take the necessary steps to request forgiveness for debts owed and to forgive others' debts.[31] For a Christian, with or without mental health concerns, an accurate perspective of forgiveness and reconciliation is essential in properly relating to God and interacting with other people, believers in Christ and unbelievers alike.

The forgiveness literature, focusing primarily on individualistic perspectives and consequently presenting a therapeutic bias, spends significant effort addressing the personal benefits achieved through forgiveness. These therapeutic benefits, which serve to motivate the offended to forgive, are of limited value to a Christian, especially in light of the apostle Paul's statement "I consider everything a loss compared to the surpassing greatness of knowing Christ Jesus my Lord" (Phil. 3:8). Moreover, major contributors in the field cite other motives which include the welfare of others, and, to a lesser extent, one's relationship with God. However, being motivated to forgive for purely humanistic reasons runs counter to a God-centered understanding of forgiveness. True biblical forgiveness has God as the primary motive since God's love is the starting point, the source, and the goal of forgiveness.

Therefore, forgiveness motivated by mere personal reasons or even for the sake of the relationship, is associated with a superficially created self-love. Personal rewards received for altruistic love, though somewhat fulfilling in terms of life experiences, do not fulfill the requirements for God-centered love for neighbors and enemies. Furthermore, purely therapeutic motives to forgive fall short of God's design for several reasons: the God-given purposes of suffering associated with

God's redemptive work are missed; the eternal rewards of true forgiveness are not recognized; and ultimately, the forgiveness offered does not fulfill God's law of love.

One final Scripture quoted from *The Message* summarizes the Christian mandate to forgive: "Live creatively, friends. If someone falls into sin, forgivingly restore him, saving your critical comments for yourself. You might be needing forgiveness before the day is out. Stoop down and reach out to those who are oppressed. Share their burdens, and so complete Christ's law. If you think you are too good for that, you are badly deceived" (Gal. 6:1).

FOLLOW-UP AND PRACTICE FOR PART THREE CONFLICT RESOLUTION

Healing the whole person often works in two directions simultaneously; one direction is "vertical," between man and God, working on changing the inner person. The other is "horizontal," between persons, working on changing the fruits of the relationships. In most cases, the more "healed" that offended individual has become (because of the vertical issues being worked out individually with God first), the more "healed" the horizontal relationships can become. It is also true that, individuals having experienced significant healing (perhaps both vertically and horizontally) can play a key role in helping other people in their process of healing. Sometimes a counselor, mentor, father/mother in the faith can make a huge difference in helping tear down walls of imprisonment. It has been said that just as people are wounded (offended) in relationship, it is in relationship, people are healed.

Life does not always present us with a specific offender. Sometimes circumstances (such as natural disasters or accidents) create hurts in our hearts that are difficult to explain. Although the Holy Spirit is our best comforter in the time of grief and loss, another person coming along side can make all the difference in the world in processing the hurt.

If reading and reflecting on this material has uncovered an area(s) of your life that needs more healing, I encourage you to seek help. Once your heart begins to receive a healing flow from heaven, it creates a hunger and thirst for more. The more healed you become, the more you realize your need for more healing. That is true in my own life, and many people I know. I would like to encourage leaders in particular to "lead" in this matter of forgiveness and reconciliation. In order to be change agents, we must become changed agents. We have nothing to give that we haven't first received/experienced from the Lord.[32] Some unique challenges exist for leaders in seeking personal healing. I recommend a book called *Sacrifice the Leader* by Paul Cox.[33]

For instances of offense where a specific offender is evident, it is surprising how many Christians believe they are justified in holding anger towards an offending person. Unresolved anger towards other people blocks healing and perpetuates conflict. The source of this anger is usually one of the excuses for unforgiveness listed in Part One Follow-up and Practice. We also discussed the problem of denial in blocking acknowledgement and repentance for a sinful response to being offended. In order for anger not to become sin, we must be willing to allow anger to be the messenger it is meant to be. After acknowledging a wrong has occurred, and recognizing that the wrong has created an obligation for repayment, the process continues with a choice to release the offender from the obligation and to cover the loss (without the help of the offender).[34] This includes surrendering the desire for vengeance or right to justice, and involves releasing feelings of anger, bitterness, and resentment toward the person.

Author Lewis Smedes discusses the relationship between anger and hate.[35] Anger from an offense turns into hatred towards the offender. A common teaching among Christians is to "love the sinner and hate the sin."[36] An offended person's mind, however, has difficulty separating offenders' actions from their person. "We attach our feelings to the moment when we were hurt, endowing it with immortality. And we let it assault us every time it comes to mind. It travels with us, sleeps with us, hovers over us while we make love …for it is a parasite sucking our blood, not theirs."[37] As Smedes also points out, it is often those a person loves the most who end up being hated the most:

> We usually hate someone who is close to us—close enough to love. We hate the person we trusted to be on our side, the person we expected to be loyal, the person we trusted to keep a promise.

> We do not usually hate strangers. We get angry at strangers. At baseball games I have raged at the cross-eyed umpire and gotten mad at the loud drunk sitting near me. But I have never hated an umpire I didn't know personally, or a drunk I never saw again. The only time we really hate strangers is when they get close enough to violate us intimately.

> Hate for people within our circle of committed love is the most virulent kind. It does not affect us so much when we hate a person who never promised to be with us, never walked with us on our private paths, never played the strings of our soul. But when a person destroys what

our commitment and our intimacy created, something precious is destroyed.[38]

Forgiveness is the only remedy to such a condition. As discussed in detail in Chapter Three, forgiveness is God's ultimate expression of love to mankind, and it is man's chief expression of love for their fellow man. A Christian does not have the option of holding unforgiveness in his heart. Choosing Christ is choosing the practice of forgiveness. Forgiveness is the ultimate expression of faith in Christ. "We love because he first loved us. Whoever claims to love God yet hates a brother or sister is a liar."[39]

Nazi Germany martyr Dietrich Bonhoeffer also reminds us in his book *Cost of Discipleship* that attempted reconciliation is mandatory for a follower of Christ. "There is therefore only one way of following Jesus and of worshipping God, and that is to be reconciled with our brethren. If we come to hear the Word of God and receive the sacrament without first being reconciled with our neighbors, we shall come to our own damnation." (Bonhoeffer 1959, 129).

When offended persons forgive someone for hurting them, they allow God to perform spiritual surgery inside their soul; He cuts away the wrong that was done to them (through Christ's sacrificial death) so that they can see their "enemy" through the redeemed eyes that can heal their soul. As people forgive their offenders, they gradually come to see more clearly the truth about them; a truth their hate blinds them to, a truth that can be seen only when the offender is separated from what they did to their victim. The truth is that those who hurt others are themselves weak, needy, and fallible human beings. They needed help, support, and comfort before they did the wrong; and they need it still. New insight can bring new feeling. When forgiving helps people see the truth about their enemies, it produces new feelings toward them.[40]

Some of the most pointed examples of this in Scripture might be the gospel accounts of how Jesus taught his lessons to the Pharisees. An example is the woman caught in adultery described in John 8. "Now in the Law Moses commanded us to stone such women; what then do you say?" (v. 5) Jesus gave them some time to gloat in their supposed superiority and then eventually said, "He who is without sin among you, let him be the first to throw a stone at her." (v. 7) Jesus gave them some more time to think about it and finally their reasoning power had to submit to their hearts. "They began to go out one by one, beginning with the older ones, and he was left alone, and the woman, where she was, in the center of the court. Straightening up, Jesus said to her, "Woman, where are they? Did no one condemn you?" She said, "No one, Lord." And Jesus said, "I do not condemn you either. Go. From now on sin no more" (vv. 9-11). What a jail break from the cycle of offense!

This newly derived insight may also take the form of recognizing lack of innocence on the part of the person offended. Engrained patterns of behavior may create opportunities for offense, and lure an unsuspecting person into an offense by means of a so-called self-fulfilling prophecy. An offended person must be willing to examine himself for any part of the offense he may be responsible for.[41] Our "offendedness" (imprisoned heart condition) may aid to capture and imprison others.

Especially true in marriage, partners are called on to relate to their spouse at a level of intimacy not experienced before marriage. If they have a bitter root of never having learned how to receive nurture from another person, they will not know how to receive love even when it is lovingly offered. Neither will they know how to give love and cherish another. They will likely avoid intimacy, withhold affection, and not recognize sincere caring when their spouse reaches out to them. They may expect rejection, coldness, and manipulation. They may be suspicious or perhaps cynical about expressions of affection. Thus their bitter roots spring up to defile the marital relationship and the entire family structure.[42] Sandford states, "Our bitter root structure can be so deep and so hidden that we are not even aware of its presence. Yet, we continually drink harm that can negatively impact the lives of those around us and eventually destroy us. Every one of us has hundreds of bitter roots which affect our attitudes and behavior."[43]

When experiencing problems, couples generally wait much too long to seek help. The presenting issues of finances, communication, etc., are most often symptoms of more root issues like those described above. Hence, each spouse being willing to separately work on his or her own "bitter root" issues is key to making it possible for the relationship to improve. When one spouse has an identified problem such as a mental health diagnosis, addiction, background of trauma, or some sort of weakness in character, the other spouse may feel justified in requiring the "problem spouse" to "straighten up," "go on meds," or "get clean" before they are willing to admit a role in the problems. Demanding change in a spouse as a prerequisite for self-change hinders the "problem" spouse's personal recovery, and stale mates any possibility for the relationship to grow.

This principle is also true in church and community relationships (as discussed in Part Three). Reconciliation can only happen between parties who really want it. It cannot be forced. Each party must be willing to look inside themselves to discover their personal blocks and surrender to God the right to judge the situation and persons involved.

If you have been injured by people you are supposed to be in "Christian fellowship" with, you have an obligation to try to make things right. After allowing God to work forgiveness in your own heart, then you can be in a position to attempt to approach your offender(s). With godly attitudes and motivations you are releasing the indebtedness, and allowing the work of Christ to be accomplished.

Isolation is one of the greatest enemies of breaking the cycle of offense. When you've been hurt, it is tempting to withdraw and try to protect yourself from being hurt again. But as you become healed in your ability to trust God, and healed in your ability to discern between trustworthy and untrustworthy people, it is time to step out and practice your healing. Allowing yourself to participate in socially "safe places" you are not necessarily comfortable in, will help you taste (or test) the fruit of forgiveness. After all, if you are now trusting Christ to have accomplished forgiveness for those who offended/offend you, you now have a Refuge to run to in the time of trouble.[44] When you feel hurt or wounded by someone's words or deeds, go back to God in the secret place, process with Him what's going on in your heart, and try once again to break down the wall of isolation. "In repentance and rest is your salvation; in quietness and trust is your strength."[45] By letting go of your own ability to control people and situations, and resting in what Christ has accomplished, your spirit quietly trusts God to give you the strength to repeat this cycle of Refuge. You have now traded your cycle of offense for a cycle of Refuge of Healing and Hope!

Free at last! Free at last! Thank God Almighty, we are free at last!

Questions for Reflection Part Three

Please refer to the Study Guide at the end of the book for the study questions in Sessions 7, 8, 9, and 10.

Hear My Heart O Lord, to Forgive

Lord, help me receive your Gift
The gift of love so divine
You paid my debt and cleanse my soul
You free from sin; my brother's and mine.

Lord, help me receive your Choice
To yield my will to your desire
Tracing anger and fear to its source
Turn from judgment, to release the mire.

Lord, help me receive your Fruit
Thoughts toward my offenders, reformed
Actions, into love transformed
Emotions renewed, and transformed.

Lord, help me receive your Forgiveness
The Gift, the Choice, and the Fruit
So Father's will be done on earth
The eagle's strength renewed in rest.

In repentance and rest is your salvation
In quietness and trust is your strength
The prophet Isaiah heard your voice
Now with blocks removed,
Let me hear and see *You* for who you really are!

Edward Hersh 3-5-2011
http://healing.bluerockbnb.com

APPENDIX A—ADDITIONAL RESOURCES

Many techniques of listening prayer, healing prayer, prayer counseling, etc. focus on various aspects and elements of "hearing God" and receiving revelation from the Holy Spirit. Many fine resources exist to aid in working through various obstacles of healing and helping people fine true refuge in Jesus. See the bibliography for some of these resources. Here is a generically simple way to invite God to heal a particularly painful memory. If you feel overwhelmed or overcome by intense emotions, my warning would be to stop and wait until you can find a trained and experienced counselor in these matters.

Basic Memory Healing Prayer Steps:

1. Acknowledge the beliefs of your inner heart and feel the emotions they stir. (i.e. I am not loved, a mistake, worthless, stupid, shameful, alone, incompetent, ...)

2. Ask Jesus to take you to the source of these ingrained beliefs.

3. Confess belief(s) (lies) in the memory (ies) and acknowledge inability to change without the help of Jesus.

4. Ask Jesus to reveal His presence in your pain in whatever way He chooses.

5. Receive Father God, Jesus, and Holy Spirit's ministry in the memory.

6. Follow through with the forgiveness self-examination exercise above for any persons discovered who have disappointed, mistreated, betrayed, or abused you.

7. Thank God for your healing and declare the truth.

APPENDIX A

A Prayer of Forgiveness

Lord Jesus, thank you for dying on the Cross and the work you completed in being the sacrifice for sin and paying the debt for my wrongdoing. You accomplished forgiveness once and for all. I now receive the words of Psalm 32 which says, "Blessed is the one whose transgressions are forgiven, whose sins are covered."

I wish to acknowledge, confess, and repent for any part of, and all guilt created by, the bitterness, resentment, and blame I have used to deny the hurt in my heart towards my offender(s). Thank you, Lord, for setting me free.

I let go of the things I have used to control people and circumstances to meet my expectations (list specific things if known) _____. I now trust You Father God to be strong in my weakness, and I surrender to you the right to judge my offender(s) and their actions.

Lord, I forgive (specific person[s]) _____ for (specific offense[s]) _____.

By your grace Lord, I will no longer wrongly judge (list persons if known) _____ for their intentional or unintentional actions that hurt me. I trust you to be the righteous Judge ruling with perfect justice and perfect mercy. I give up ruminating, blaming, justifying, and all forms of denying the truth about this situation(s).

Father God, where I have perceived you responsible for the pain I feel; forgive me for wrongly judging you. Where I have falsely blamed myself, condemned myself, or hated things about myself that you created me to be, forgive me.

Lord, heal my spirit, mind, soul, and body. Wash me clean as I jail break the debtor's prison. I declare myself whole, released from any torment my enemy would seek to imprison me in. Christ has forgiven. I am forgiven. I forgive as He has forgiven.

Amen.

Note: This is a sample prayer by Dr. Ed Hersh, Blue Rock BnB Healing Ministry

A Prayer for Family Line Sin

O Lord, I acknowledge you as the Father of my family of origin. Since the creation of Adam and Eve, You have continued to reveal your divine purposes for families on the earth. Both blessing and cursing have come down through the generations.

(*If you have been adopted, thank God for your adoptive family as well and continue.*)

I thank You for the blessings coming through my family line _____ (list the ones that come to mind; e.g. gift of life, talents ...). Where I have failed to receive Your blessing through my family line, I repent today and ask you to help me change

... _____ (list areas where you have become aware this is true). Where my family and I have forgotten God, and neglected to praise Him for His wonderful deeds, I repent.

I thank you, Lord, for the family you have placed me in. I thank you for my parents. In those areas where I have dishonored my parents/ ancestors _____ (list all that come to mind), I ask You Lord to forgive me, and help me to give honor and fulfill your holy commandment to do so. I choose not to blame my parents for their shortcomings and failures. The hurts to me that may have resulted because of things they did or didn't do, I place now at the cross of Jesus Christ for Him to wash clean and heal. I choose to forgive my parents for any ways _____ (list) they have dishonored me, and I ask You Lord to help me honor the children, and children's children you give to me to continue the family line.

As the Father of our family, forgive us Lord for the things my family and I have done to dishonor you, thus bringing a curse in place of blessing. Break off these curses and restore blessing, so that the generations to come will know you and honor you for who you are. Where my family and I have broken covenant with God, been distrustful toward God, acted stubbornly, complained, and become rebellious, disloyal, or unfaithful, please forgive us/ me for these actions and heart attitudes ... _____

(List all that come to mind, or pause and ask Him to reveal specifics of family patterns.)

Some typical patterns:

Diseases, divorce, prejudices, ungodly judgments, sexual sins (incest, molestation, immorality), addictions (alcohol, drugs, porn), family secrets, denial, occult activity, uncontrolled anger, fear, abandonment, invalidation, shame, hopelessness, confusion, victimization, self-rejection.

Thank you, Father for not treating me as my sins deserve. Thanks for preparing your path to life through Jesus Christ. As I have confessed the sins above, I trust Jesus to be faithful and just, cleansing me from all unrighteousness.

Through Jesus Christ, I now declare all things made right, and the curses through my family line cut off. I proclaim healing and restoration of God's purposes for family in my life and the land I live. I thank you, Lord, for the power of the Holy Spirit to renew my mind and heart.

Amen.

NOTE: This sample prayer is offered by Dr. Ed Hersh based on Psalm78. (http://healing.bluerockbnb.com)

A Prayer for Self-Rejection/Self-Blame Forgiveness

Father God, in the Name of Jesus, I ask you to forgive me for _____

(All that apply: self-doubt, self-condemnation, self-blame, self-rejection, self-hate, self-righteousness, self-destruction, false guilt).

I choose to forgive myself for _____ (all the above). I rest in Christ's salvation to release me from guilt or shame because of these sins. In the Name of Jesus, I cancel all of Satan's authority to accuse me or torment me concerning this sin. I refuse the lie of the enemy that this act made me unclean, unlovable or not valuable. God has forgiven me and covered this sin because of Jesus Christ's redemptive work on the cross. Holy Spirit, come and heal my heart of the ungodly beliefs and false guilt. Tell me the truth about this situation.

In the name of Jesus and the power of your blood, I command this spirit of self-rejection to go.

Thank you, Lord, for freedom this day. Amen.

Lord, I now see that self-rejection and self-bitterness led me to resentment and retaliation (and perhaps even violence) against myself. I thought I was so right because I was trying to prevent others from being harmed or injured. But I did not trust you to be a strong God who can take care of the things I was trying to control. I thought of myself as strong, and so I hated myself for the weakness of not being able to measure up.

I blamed myself for things out of my control. I now forgive myself for taking on responsibility for loads I was not meant to carry. I choose to rest in Jesus' ability to prevent this sin. Forgive me for the stress and burden that I inflicted upon my body and soul. Repair my heart, soul, mind, and body by your grace. I declare that you alone are the righteous judge and I am surrendered to your opinion of me and others.

Amen.

Note: This is a sample prayer by Dr. Ed Hersh, Blue Rock BnB Healing Ministry/Light of Hope CSO.

APPENDIX A

Negative Feelings/Emotion Category List with Psalms

I highly recommend the Psalms as a tool to find refuge. If you have a Bible, simply open it to the middle and you will likely land on one of the 150 Psalm. The writers of the Psalms struggled with the everyday problems of the human condition. They show how to overcome. They even point to the only Savior and Lord who appeared about 1,000 years after they were written. Jesus Christ fulfills the Psalms' heart cry in a human/ divine sort of intervention. Now as we look back 2,000 years on Christ's fulfillment, the Holy Spirit reveals powerful solutions (Refuge) to any spiritual or emotional struggle we face. Here is a list of some negative feelings you may be experiencing, and a Psalm to connect with Refuge. This list is not scientific and not exhaustive, but it comes out of my own personal journey of finding help in the time of trouble (Ps. 46). The numbers below correspond to Psalm numbers.

Abandonment (deserted, discarded, forgotten, left out, lost ...)

| Psalm | 3 | 10 | 22 | 31 | 38:1-16 64:1-6 | 69 |
| 77 88 | 102:3-11 | | 109:1-5 137 | 142:1-4 | | |

Confusion (bewildered, confused, dumb founded, indecisive, indifferent...)

| Psalm | 10 | 22 | 38 | 73 | 77 | **88** |
| 102:3-11 | | | | | | |

Fear (agitated, anxious, desperate, fearful, hysterical, nervous, scared, suspicious, terror, untrusting ...)

Psalm	18	22	27	31	55:1-11 56
57:4-6	59:1-7 64:1-6	88		109:1-5	116:3
142:6	143:3-4				

Hopelessness (defeated, hopeless, fatigued ....)

Psalm 10 22 31 38 56 57:4-6
69:1-21 88 102:3-11 116:3 119:25-28 137
142 143:3-4

Invalidation (belittled, betrayed, disgraced, inferior, insignificant, unappreciated, unloved ...)

Psalm 22:6-7 31 38 41:7-9 55:1-11
69:1-21 73 88 109:1-5 116:3 119:25-28
137 142 143:3-4

Powerlessness (confined, cornered, defenseless, frail, helpless, impotent, oppressed, weak ...)

Psalm 3 7 22 31 38 56
57:4-6 59:1-7 64:1-6 77 88 102:3-11
109:1-5, 22-25 116:3 119:25-28 137 142
143:3-4

Shame (ashamed, bad, depraved, disloyal, failure, fault, indecent, stupid, trashy, unclean...)

Psalm 12 22 38:1-16 44:15 51:3-6
69:1-21 123 129:1-4 137

142:1-4

Tainted (crazy, careless, damaged, flawed, ruined, screwed up, wasted ...)

Psalm 19:12-13 22:67 64:1-6 69:1-21 73 88
102:3-11 123 137 142 143:3-4

Revengeful Emotions (depressed, angry, hate, critical, judgmental, bitterness, strife, defiant, violent ...)

Psalm 22 31 35 52 56:7 58
69:22-28 73 109:6-21 137:8-9

140:9-11

Appendix B—Author's Personal Story and Healing Journey

As one of those Christians who cannot account for a specific day when I converted to Christ, most of my life has been a journey of following Jesus since I was a young boy. My religious experience is scattered across the denominational spectrum. Near the time when I married, we became founding members in a church we believed was on the cutting edge of church life, following a model of radical obedience to God's word for us as believers. A popular verse in our movement came from Acts 13:36 which says, "David had served God's purpose in his own generation." We served God with great zeal in order to "do whatever your hand finds to do, for God is with you." (1 Sam 10:7). I am deeply grateful to God for my loving parents and the fellow sojourners we have grown within the faith over the years. However, even the greatest amount of zeal for God cannot overcome a fundamental inability to receive God's love caused by obstacles such as core misbeliefs (lies believed about oneself, God, and others), wounds, and social injustice.

In 1998 I was introduced to a book called *The Transformation of the Inner Man* by John and Paula Sandford. The teachings of the Elijah House based on this book brought an enormous amount of healing to my body, soul, and spirit. Even having been in churches where the "baptism in the Spirit" was practiced, I was met by the Holy Spirit in a new way that validated emotional connection to a loving God. My picture of God changed and I heard His voice differently. I answered a call of God to pursue more training in counseling and healing ministry. My career had been in software development so I took a job at Regent University in Virginia Beach, VA, so I could study in their graduate school. I completed an MA degree in Human Service Counseling and then entered a doctoral program at Trinity Theological Seminary in Newburgh, IN. Also, through self study, I investigated what seems to be every ministry, method, and book on the topic of inner healing.

About the time I was choosing a topic for my major writing project to culminate the Doctor of Religious Studies degree (I completed it in 2010), an event occurred that clearly placed forgiveness at the center of all I had studied and experienced the last twelve years. A youth in our community shot and killed Mike and Kathy Borden, the parents of his fourteen-year-old girlfriend, on November 13, 2005. The families on both sides of the tragedy are Christians. Then ten months later, Carl Roberts, a local man, also from a Christian family background, premeditated a crime against innocent Amish children in which ten people were killed or injured in a fit of rage. "Peaceful" Lancaster County, PA became the scene of heinous crime committed by "Christian" people. These were not your stereotypical "thugs" from the "inner city." Other similar crimes occurred before and some since, but these struck close to home because our family connections are close. Besides the deaths, the aftermath is ugly. I cannot explore it here, but many questions still remain. God provides at least one answer—forgiveness, if we can get our heads and hearts around it.

Anger, hate, and rage do not "just happen." Jesus points this out in Matthew 5:21-23. It's a progression. Unrighteously judging (wrongly forming an opinion of) another person, ruminating, and failure to surrender to God are all elements of something I call a cycle of offense (explained in Chapter One). Since Jesus defines anger as simply calling someone a "fool," he is making the point that ALL of us are guilty of denying hatred, lust, and other ungodly passions that can lead to disastrous results.

"There, but for the grace of God, go I" (John Bradford). This sixteenth century martyr helps me gain perspective. Like every human being, innate sin has caused me to struggle with "bad fruit" and "bad roots" in my life. Unrighteous anger is a "fruit" with which I am well acquainted. Bad roots have surfaced and been dealt with (with more likely to appear). Though it's God's grace that I haven't behaved in a way that would make me a criminal (in a physical sense), it is also God's grace that I haven't had to stay in the imprisonment of cycles of self-defeat, self-rejection, performance-based living, victim-predator, depression, anxiety and others. Through Jesus Christ I am a jail breaker, no longer a jail bird. I am a "free bird" (emphasis on the free, not the bird)!

Freedom in spirit and soul does not necessarily translate into freedom from adversity and struggle in circumstances of life. In fact, like many, I find just the opposite to be true. The scriptural principle holds true that the more knowledge one gains in a matter, the greater responsibility one shares in acting appropriately on the understanding received. Since healing usually involves working through some sort of pain, more gain, may mean more pain. "Consider it pure joy, my brothers and sisters, whenever you face trials of many kinds, because you know that the testing of your faith produces perseverance. Let perseverance finish its work so that you may be mature and complete, not lacking anything" (James 1:2-4).

On the positive side, I have found that healing begets healing. The more "healed" I become, the more my heart desires the transparency with God to bring more healing. Having become knowledgeable on the topic of forgiveness, has certainly come with its "testing." What I've written in the book is only a measure of what I've learned, but I want to share as much as I'm able to communicate so that others can also benefit from my pain (and joy). The greatest end, of course, is to glorify Almighty God and enjoy His Presence forever.

My background also contains some significant "stuff" created by a condition of optic nerve damage at birth. Legal blindness has presented challenges (and produced perseverance) that I could write an entire book about someday. I lived my childhood with the receiving end of "kids can be cruel." In adolescence I blamed a lot on God and questioned the typical "hard things in life to understand" with the added burden of trying to figure out what society means by "normal." Adulthood intensified this struggle as I tried to fulfill duties of manhood (husband, father of four, employee, leader, etc) like other men, but with less than half the eyesight of a person seeing with 20/20 vision. Without a driver's license, severely limited access to printed material, and handicaps in social settings, I was (and am) forced to depend on God who came through in numerous and miraculous ways. My theme verse became the passage in 2 Corinthians 10:9-12 which says, "But he said to me, "My grace is sufficient for you, for my power is made perfect in weakness." Therefore I will boast all the more gladly about my weaknesses, so that Christ's power may rest on me. That is why, for Christ's sake, I delight in weaknesses, in insults, in hardships, in persecutions, in difficulties. For when I am weak, then I am strong."

Escaping the Pain of Offense

As a person with a disability I identify closely with people in underprivileged classes. Society's attitude towards people with disabilities is generally demeaning and lacking inclusively. People with disabilities are generally viewed as "needy" only, instead of valuable contributors who possess a piece of what is needed for the community as a whole to thrive. Unfortunately, the Church seems to be as guilty as the society at large in the failure to provide people with disabilities dignity, opportunity, equality and empowerment. If the civil rights struggle to improve conditions for people with disability is compared to the civil rights movement of the '60s—Rosa Parks being asked to give up her seat on the bus for a white person— might be compared to a person with a disability being told they shouldn't be trying to board the bus. Lack of employment opportunities, poverty, and social isolation are common place and at much higher rates among this group than the public at large. There are some wonderful people doing some great things to address these problems. I would be remiss in failing to acknowledge and thank these persons. On the other hand, much of the assistance offered is patronizing because it fails to include the participation and contributions of persons with disabilities themselves.

By default, as a member of the "disability community," I have become an advocate forced to take occasionally unpopular positions on matters in the community at large. Again, this is not a position I would choose, but by God's grace I can help others bear their burden, to some degree at least. I mention all this because participation in society as part of an "oppressed class" creates even more opportunities to understand and practice the grace of forgiveness.

Jesus' teachings consistently contrasted the physical realm with the spiritual. Most of the physical healings recorded in the gospels were performed with a direct message of spiritual healing. Jesus healed peoples' eyesight to demonstrate the spiritual blindness of people of the day (particularly the religious). Our generation is no less "blind." We are blind to the bitterness, resentment and blame in our hearts. Even God's people are often blind to the power of forgiveness, and the world of freedom waiting outside the walls of the prison of darkness. "The most pathetic person in the world is someone who has sight but has no vision" (Helen Keller).

Most profoundly, Jesus communicates this in the story of the man born blind that is healed in John chapter nine. I think many miss the main point of the story explained in the last few verses.

> "Jesus said 'For judgment I have come into this world, so that the blind will see and those who see will become blind.' Some Pharisees who were with him heard him say this and asked, 'What? Are we blind too?' Jesus said, 'If you were blind, you would not be guilty of sin; but now that you claim you can see, your guilt remains.'" (John 9:39-41)

Blindness is the spiritual condition of those unable to surrender to God the right to judge the guilt of offense. Jesus opens spiritual eyes. Jesus only frees those from debtor's prison who first see their captive condition. Those who think they see well enough without Christ's intervention, are doomed to a life characterized by blindness. The parts of our heart not yet surrendered to Christ for *His* judgment will grow like a cataract gradually creating greater degrees of blindness. There is no neutral territory. We allow the eyes of our heart to be opened wider to God's message of forgiveness, overtaking the darkness, or we choose to close the eyes of our heart (being content in unforgiveness), surrendering to darkness.

In the story mentioned above the physically blind man was accused by religious people of both having some sort of sin in his life, and not having enough faith to be healed (physically). They became trapped into thinking their physical sight qualified them to judge the "blind" man's spiritual condition. Hence Jesus warned, "now that you claim you can see, your guilt remains." Jesus was interested in healing the "whole person." Understanding and practicing forgiveness is the centerpiece of spiritual vision and peoples' freedom in Christ. I have experienced an incredible amount of healing in my own life. As I have allowed God (Father, Son and Holy Spirit) to change my heart from the inside out, my responses to life circumstances improve; past, present and future. Triggers from past hurts no longer have the intensity they once did. Fellowship with God is more intimate because many blocks have been removed. The future looks brighter as God multiplies the seeds of my repentance (from ungodly judgments) to yield an increased harvest of good fruit.

Presently I am involved in a number of arenas to try to make a difference and advocate for "whole person" healing. A number of years ago I connected with a medical doctor in Lancaster who has similar apparition to combine a spiritual approach alongside the typical medical treatment to physical, mental and emotional health problems. Robert Doe, MD leads a ministry called Light of Hope Community Service Organization. I am part of a team of counselors who works with Dr. Doe in clinic settings to provide spiritual care treatment for illnesses, addictions and mental health issues. This project is called the Refuge of Healing and Hope and consists of people from various churches and ministries in our community. I serve other organizations in chaplaincy work, and serve on mission teams to promote transformation and healing of the whole person.

Lancaster County is a popular tourist area in Pennsylvania. My wife and I operate Blue Rock Bed and Breakfast to welcome visitors and provide lodging and breakfast to guests from all over the world. In addition to the hospitality, some people come to our location for healing ministry. I offer individual and family counseling from a spiritual perspective. Particularly for leaders, this affords an opportunity to receive help without the risks of exposing problems in their local community. Part of this ministry is also training to help leaders and lay counseling teams sharpen their skills in prayer counseling and healing ministry.

Let me extend a warm welcome for you to come visit us in Lancaster. We're conveniently located near many attractions, and if you are looking for more than a vacation, we would be honored to be a part of what God is doing in your healing journey as well!

I have gleaned the best from each of the numerous counseling and inner person healing techniques I have studied over the years, and allow the Holy Spirit to reveal and direct what is needed on a case by case basis. The tools and templates I draw from often focus on themes in this book.

You can find information on our websites (e.g. search for items like my name with Blue Rock Bed and Breakfast Healing Ministry). You can also search for the author's blog to continue learning more and discussing topics related to God-centered forgiveness, mental health, and conflict resolution.

Appendix C—Overcoming an Abortion

"... I wish I would have understood as much about abortion as I do today."

A few years ago I wish I would have understood as much about abortion as I do today. When I was eighteen years old I became pregnant, and like many other girls, I went to Planned Parenthood for a pregnancy test. The father (who is now my husband) insisted on an abortion. I wanted to have the baby. I was so scared I didn't even tell my parents. The Planned Parenthood counselor also steered me towards abortion. This left me feeling alone and helpless.

In a pre-abortion group counseling session at the abortion facility, I was made to feel abnormal because I wanted to have my baby. Unable to withstand the pressure, I went through with the abortion.

My husband later realized what he did and we both regretted it ever since. I asked myself questions like "What kind of child did I destroy?" or "What would he have grown up to be?" I realize now that I killed a child, a child who had been moving inside of me since conception, who had a heartbeat and had developed internal organs.

As a Christian, I came to see that abortion is wrong in God's eyes and I had to take responsibility for my actions. I realized that God was with me at the time, wanting to give me His strength to help me make it through my pregnancy. I was just too scared to reach out for His hand. My husband and I asked for God's forgiveness and He has forgiven us. If you have had an abortion, He cares, loves and will forgive you.

—Jerri—

Are you hurting because of an abortion?

If you know more than you did when it happened, you may feel a burdensome guilt from the experience. Maybe it's even worse, to the point of feeling emotionally drained. You may be feeling terrible about yourself for what you did; feeling angry, depressed or even bitter towards doctors, counselors, a boyfriend or parents who "pushed" you into it. Whatever pain you are experiencing, you are not alone. Many women are struggling with the same fears. Some, like Jerri, have worked through their difficulties and have found hope to turn a desperate situation around.

The grief you may feel is a healthy sign that you are facing reality and not suppressing feelings that will only get worse the longer they fester inside you. The first step to being healed from emotional wounds is to admit the wounds exist and realize the cause of the wounds. You may have been told by doctors, abortion facility counselors or other "family planning" personnel that the grief you are feeling is abnormal. You may have been made to feel foolish, selfish or simply confused about the whole thing.

The grief you feel is not abnormal! It is indeed normal. When you become pregnant your body prepares biologically and emotionally for the baby. When the baby is taken away, the processes of preparation are interrupted and the loss is felt.

Life is a gift from God. God is the Creator of all life. An unborn baby is a unique expression of God's creative ability, possessing just as much life in the womb as in adulthood. Since God tells us not to destroy life which he has created (Exod. 21:13), abortion is sin, but the good news follows.

Sin separates us from God, not allowing us to receive what God has for us in life. Jesus Christ died on the cross so that we would have a way to be freed from the power of sin and be reunited with God. Jesus said, "I am the way, the truth and the life." (John 14:6). By putting our trust in the fact that Jesus is "the way" we can make Him the Lord (ruler) of our life. It is after we relinquish the control of our life to Him that He can do something with it, Jesus said, "If anyone wishes to come after Me, let him deny himself, and take up his cross and follow Me. For whoever wishes to save his life shall lose it; but whoever loses his life for My sake shall find it" (Matt. 16: 24, 25).

God is not mad or angry at *you* for aborting your baby, or for anything else you may have done (no matter how bad you think it is). God hates sin but He loves people and desires to forgive them of sin. He is standing with open arms to receive you and forgive you. He wants to give you the power to live a clean life, free from guilt and shame.

If you have aborted a baby, or encouraged someone else to do so, God will forgive you right now if you ask Him to. The Bible says, "If we confess our sins, He is faithful and just to forgive us our sins and to cleanse us from all unrighteousness" (1 John 1:9).

Through God's forgiveness you can experience true freedom from whatever is troubling you. By receiving God's forgiveness in your own life, you can turn around and extend that forgiveness to whomever you may feel anger or resentment towards for helping *to* cause your problems.

Let God take you through this healing process. You can feel good about yourself, and a brand new life of peace and fulfillment can be yours.

We realize that sometimes in working through your feelings you may need someone to talk to, so if we can help you in any way please call the person who gave you this pamphlet or:

Note: The text above is the contents of a pamphlet written by the Hershes nearly thirty years ago. Thousands of copies were distributed throughout the globe and several translations created in other languages.

Study Guide

CONTENTS of the STUDY GUIDE

Comments and Cautions for Group Study

Within each Session below are listed the sections of the *Escaping the Pain of Offense* book that are covered in the respective study session (based on 10 sessions).

Session One
Beginning **Part One** of the book
Foreword by Dr. Robert Doe
Preface
Chapter 1 — Introduction: The Cycle of Offense
Follow–up and Practice for Part One – Foundations

Session Two
Chapter 2 — Forgiveness: Misunderstandings
Follow–up and Practice for Part One – Foundations

Session Three
Chapter 3 — Forgiveness: Divinely Initiated
Follow–up and Practice for Part One – Foundations

Session Four
Beginning **Part Two** of the book
Chapter 4 — Forgiveness: Receiving God's Gift

Follow–up and Practice for Part Two – Transformational Healing

Session Five
Chapter 5 — Forgiveness: Surrendering to God
Follow–up and Practice for Part Two – Transformational Healing

Session Six
Chapter 6 — Forgiveness: Trusting God for Change
Follow–up and Practice for Part Two – Transformational Healing

Session Seven
Beginning **Part Three** of the book
Chapter 7 — Forgiveness and Reconciliation
Follow–up and Practice for Part Three – Conflict Resolution

Session Eight
Chapter 8 — Reconciliation in Relationships
Follow–up and Practice for Part Three – Conflict Resolution

Session Nine
Chapter 9 — Conclusion Part I
Follow–up and Practice for Part Three – Conflict Resolution

Session Ten
Chapter 9 — Conclusion Part II
Follow–up and Practice for Part Three – Conflict Resolution
Appendix A – Resources and sample prayers
Appendix B – Author's Personal Story and Healing Journey
Appendix C – Overcoming an Abortion

Comments and Cautions for Group Study

Study Groups reading *Escaping the Pain of Offense: Empowered to Forgive from the Heart* can benefit greatly through accompanying the content with discussion and prayer support. The text in each chapter and the follow-up and practice content at the end of each Part can serve as the basis for exploring the topic of forgiveness together in a group setting. The number of sessions allowed to process through the book can vary depending on the goals and objectives for outcomes. For example, a very brief overview can be achieved in three sessions with each of the three Parts of the book become the subject of a session. Six sessions could be used to split the material in six parts. Eight sessions would require splitting the material in eight parts, and so forth. This guide is based on a ten session study.

A word of caution: Although more thorough examination of the material can yield deeper heart level transformation, members of a group should not be made to feel compelled to conform to a particular practice. Remember, forgiveness is first getting your heart right with God. This is an intensely "personal" matter, and individuals must be given space to process their own stuff with God. "Peer pressure" should not be used in any way to make people respond in a certain manner. Remember the "peeling and onion" illustration? Some members of a group may be ready to peel more than others. Some may be ready to yield their hearts to deeper levels of transformation. Each individual's willingness, or unwillingness, to expose their heart in a group setting must be respected.

In addition to the caution expressed above, the Group Facilitator's judgment will need to be exercised as to the specifics of how the group sessions are structured and executed. The author of this guide is assuming the Facilitator has a working understanding of group dynamics and is able to discern between healthy and unhealthy (holy and unholy) interactions of group members.

Session One — Introduction

Beginning **Part One** of the book — Foundations

Read the Following:
Foreword by Dr. Robert Doe
Preface
Chapter 1 — Introduction: The Cycle of Offense
Follow–up and Practice for Part One – Foundations

Some Key Points:

1. From the Foreword we see that the government of God ("kingdom of God") includes transformational healing as a key component. God is all about healing, and earthly governmental structures can best serve their people when favorability is extended to God-centered approaches to healing. From the broadest perspectives of our society's ability to function well, the health of a person's inner being is a core element.

2. The Preface extends this point with illustrations of how individuals' lack of self-government and lack of honoring God's government can mess up many people's lives. Mankind's desperate condition of helplessness to change without divine intervention becomes increasingly more real the closer a tragedy strikes to personal and family circumstances.

3. In Chapter 1, what the author calls the Cycle of Offense is introduced. From a Christian worldview perspective, without

God's intervention mankind is hopelessly imprisoned in a broken world characterized by sin and transgression.

4. Sessions One, Two, and Three include the Follow-up and Practice for Part One – Foundations. For Session One, the main purpose for examining this material is to help you examine your thoughts and feelings about God. It's hardly possible to have a God-centered approach to topics in the book without God being at the center of your life. This book assumes the reader already has a basic understanding of what it means to follow Christ. Becoming a disciple of Christ is the first step in growing in relationship to Father God and receiving the empowerment to *forgive from the heart*.

Session One Reflection and Discussion Questions

1. What are your thoughts and feelings about the *Foreword* of the book? Describe any similar examples/ circumstances in your personal/church/community life?

2. What are your thoughts and feelings about the *Preface* of the book? Describe any similar examples/circumstances in your personal/church/community life?

3. Is God the center of your life? Do you want Him to be the center? Who is Jesus to you?

4. Describe/evaluate your relationship with God, past and present. How has your relationship improved from when you first believed? What would you like to see improve?

5. As you read the verses in Isaiah 61 quoted at the beginning of Chapter One, how does it stir your heart?

6. Where has been, or where is the cycle of offense active in your life? Explain the events and your responses. Who or what might be stuck in unforgiveness?

7. When you are hurt, do you instinctively blame others? Do you blame yourself? Do you retaliate or ruminate? List examples.

STUDY GUIDE

Session Two — Forgiveness: Misunderstandings

Read the Following:
Chapter 2 — Forgiveness: Misunderstandings
Follow–up and Practice for Part One – Foundations

Some Key Points:

1. Biblical truth and Christians' belief and practice (in the
Church in America) sometimes seem to be on an increasingly
divergent path. Personal problems and relational conflict are
fruits of doubt and unbelief evidenced in many Christians'
lifestyles.

2. Forgiveness is one of the most important topics of which many
Christians have lost clear focus. Examining what forgiveness *is
not*, can help clarify what forgiveness *is*.

3. In order for a forgiveness intervention to be most successful
in a Christian's mental health treatment and spiritual growth,
understanding and applying a God-centered approach which
emphasizes the finished work of Christ and progressive
sanctification affords the most fruitful results.

Session Two Reflection and Discussion Questions

1. How has the lack of understanding and practice of forgiveness
kept you in bondage? Explain the circumstances or describe the
relationship results.

2. In what settings or under what circumstances do you have most difficulty recognizing your need to change? What forms of denial might be at work in these situations? (e.g. simple denial, minimizing, blaming, excusing, generalizing, dodging, or attacking etc.).

3. Are you rarely, sometimes, often, usually, or always (pick one) ready to allow your friend(s) to point out your blind spots? Explain.

4. What forms of ungodly "control" might you be confusing with the godly kind of self-discipline and self-control commanded in the Bible? In what ways might you be "the master of your fate," instead of trusting God as Refuge and Lord?

5. By reading this section, what area(s) of misunderstanding have you uncovered about forgiveness? How do you now see it?

6. In what ways are you "hard on yourself"? Use the cycle of offense to describe how you might become trapped by self-doubt, self-condemnation, self-blame, "false" guilt, or self-rejection.

7. What is your understanding of the term "absolute truth"? How do your beliefs about God factor into your answer?

8. In general, are you satisfied with your current level of biblical knowledge? What could you do (and willing to do) to become better informed?

Session Three — Forgiveness: Divinely Initiated

Read the Following:
Chapter 3 — Forgiveness: Divinely Initiated
Follow–up and Practice for Part One – Foundations

Some Key Points:

1.   Forgiveness is God's idea. Honoring God's authority in our lives must include our surrender to his purpose and plan regarding forgiveness.

2.   Forgiveness has a historical context in the Creation, Fall, Redemption, and Consummated World.

3. Jesus is the Savior, providing both perfect justice and perfect mercy for mankind. The death and resurrection of Christ has accomplished forgiveness. Christ's work is based in Father's love and now carried out by the Holy Spirit (in cooperation with mankind).

Session Three Reflection and Discussion Questions

1.   Explain what it means to say, "Christ has accomplished forgiveness."

2. Explain John 20:21-23. Also read the larger context. Again Jesus said, "Peace be with you! As the Father has sent me, I am sending you." And with that he breathed on them and said,

"Receive the Holy Spirit. If you forgive anyone his sins, they are forgiven; if you do not forgive them, they are not forgiven."
3. Reflecting on the Scripture references and points discussed in Chapter 3, name some of the things you discovered (or re-discovered) that encourage you the most about God's initiation of forgiveness.

4. How is a God-centered view of forgiveness set apart from other ways of looking at forgiveness?

5. Reflecting on the historical aspects of the life and work of Christ, can you think of Old Testament examples of "types" of Christ? Explain. How might these help us in our understanding and practice of forgiveness in our current times?

6. What amazes you the most about God being perfect justice and perfect mercy at the same time?

7. How does God define love? Explain how a person's perception of God factors into their ability to love.

Session Four — Forgiveness: Receiving God's Gift

Beginning Part Two — Transformational Healing:
A Personal Matter between Man and God

Read the Following:
Chapter 4 — Forgiveness: Receiving God's Gift
Follow–up and Practice for Part Two – Transformational Healing

Some Key Points:
1.   Two theological terms deserve clarification; justification and sanctification. The author focuses on sanctification as a key element of forgiveness, and forgiveness as a key element of sanctification.

2.   Many mental health conditions often have spiritual and emotional roots, and research shows that even many physical problems are rooted in emotional and mental health issues. Emotions are neither good nor bad, and they can be a powerful tool in exposing and clearing up faulty thinking patterns.

3.   Knowing *about* forgiveness is not enough; one must *experience* forgiveness. To practice God-centered forgiveness, one must know the Forgiver. Our heart perceptions of God determine our ability to receive His healing touch.

4.   A person's honesty and humility (regarding self) are at the center of heart transformation towards forgiveness.

Session Four Reflection and Discussion Questions

1. What is the difference between "healthiness" and "wholeness"?

2. What is the difference between "being sorry" and repenting? Site examples.

3. What is the difference between a conversion experience and being sanctified? What does this look like in your own life?

4. Reflect on Ephesians 2:8-10; What are these verses saying? What are they saying to you? How can you apply them? "For it is by grace you have been saved, through faith—and this not from yourselves, it is the gift of God—not by works, so that no one can boast. For we are God's workmanship, created in Christ Jesus to do good works, which God prepared in advance for us to do."

5. Do you make a conscious effort to define your feelings; on a scale of 1 to 10 (1 being never and 10 being always)? Explain. What are some of the feelings you feel most often?

6. Emotions are messengers carrying a message. Explain.

7. What is the difference between feelings and emotions? How do your feelings feed your emotional responses?

8. Provide some examples of how feelings and emotions are expressed in the Psalms (see Psalm reference sheet in Appendix A). Also identify in the Bible some examples of how Jesus handles feelings and emotions.

9. Other than childhood trauma, what difficult situations have you faced in life, and how have you overcome? Have you/ how have you seen God intervene on your behalf?

10. How difficult is it for you to "draw near" to God? What are some barriers of drawing closer?

11. Practice allowing your emotions to identify the source of pain, lie believed causing the pain, and the truth Jesus is speaking to bring healing. (See Basic Memory Healing Prayer sample in Appendix A.)

12. In what areas of your life do you suspect that denial is most active? How does pride keep you from being honest with yourself?

Session Five — Forgiveness: Surrendering to God

Read the Following:
Chapter 5 — Forgiveness: Surrendering to God
Follow–up and Practice for Part Two – Transformational Healing

Some Key Points:

1. The essence of forgiveness is yielding to God and releasing the offense. It is surrendering to God the right to judge a matter or reclaim debt. Forgiveness offers release to those oppressed by the sin of rejecting God's intervention and glorifying self. Yielding the offense to God and surrendering the offender to His judgment is the only way to free a Christian from holding (and re-making) an ungodly "judgment" that causes bitterness and resentment.

2. Sanctification affects both the physical and nonphysical parts of the human being. In ever-increasing measure, believers should become "obedient from the heart."

3. Releasing offenses is an important part of whole person healing from a medical and therapeutic viewpoint. Neglecting the emotional part of a person's being can have damaging consequences. Toxic stress leads to a host of medical and psychological problems.

4. Jesus did not keep the power to heal and deliver to Himself; He empowered His disciples to practice it also.

Session Five Reflection and Discussion Questions

1. Do you tend to be intellectually driven or emotionally driven? Explain. How might you become more balanced?

2. What stands in the way of you being more of a "whole person" at the present time? What needs to happen to remove that obstacle?

3. Describe the situation and why it has been so hard for you to forgive someone in your life. Write about the hurt, pain, and damage it has brought into your life.

4. Do you rehearse (in your mind) "speeches" you would like to give to someone? Do you try to avoid that person? Describe the feelings you have and what you would like to say to them.

5. Explain what it means for Christ to accomplish forgiveness (for the situation above).

6. List your major resentment. How is it interfering with your life? List situations where you became angry because of your resentments.

7. We often have a strong need to be in control. We overreact to change over which we have no control. In what area of your life do you experience the strongest need to be in control? What do you fear when you're not in control? What do you feel?

8. What specific behavior(s) is a problem you have been avoiding? Or what behavior are you defending or excusing? How do you do this? What causes you to know that you must turn your will and your life over to the care of God in this area? What steps will you take to turn it over?

Session Six — Forgiveness: Trusting God for Change

Read the Following:

Chapter 6 — Forgiveness: Trusting God for Change

Follow–up and Practice for Part Two – Transformational Healing

Some Key Points:

1. Critical judgments are the root of unforgiveness in a person's heart and unresolved conflict in relationships.

2. Forgiveness is both an event and a journey.

3. Emotions are messengers. When the message is painful, the pain should be engaged to find its true source and healing of the wound.

4. Bad fruit (undesirable behavior) comes from a bad root (undesired, hidden source). Problematic critical judgments made in the present are usually rooted in past ungodly responses and patterns formed through repetition.

5. Father God's love is the source, power, and vehicle of forgiveness. God (as he relates to mankind) is all about forgiveness, and forgiveness is all about God (John 3:16-17).

Session Six Reflection and Discussion Questions

1. Read and study Luke 6:43-45. Explain what it means. "No good tree bears bad fruit, nor does a bad tree bear good fruit. Each tree is recognized by its own fruit. People do not pick figs

from thornbushes, or grapes from briers. The good man brings good things out of the good stored up in his heart, and the evil man brings evil things out of the evil stored up in his heart. For out of the overflow of his heart his mouth speaks."

2. Are you able to discern any repetitious (and undesirable) results in events or relationships in your life? What *pattern(s)* of "dysfunction" might be most evident?

3. Explain at least one positive example and at least one negative example of the principle of "sowing and reaping" in your life.

4. Describe any unwanted fruit (negative patterns in relationships) that you feel might be connected to a bitter root from your childhood (ages 0-6 or 6-12).

5. Do you recall a condemning judgment of a parent/primary caretaker? Until now you have forgotten the judgment. It may even be a surprise to you when you connect the seed that was sown back then and the influence of this root on the fruit (behaviors) in your life today. Describe the root and the fruit as you see the connection.

(Example: Your father was in the military and at times was away for months. You judged him for not being there for you like other fathers. While you were proud of him, at the same time you were angry with him. Your being proud of him tipped the scales in choosing to marry a workaholic. Now you project the angry judgment against your father onto your husband. This anger now acts to drive your husband to be away even more than he normally would be.)

6. Think of some inner promises (vows) you have made in the past that are still affecting your thoughts and attitudes presently. How have these affected specific relationships in your life and what changes would help correct the damage?

7. Toward whom or what do you feel bitterness, anger, rage, or other forms of malice? What opinion(s) (perhaps resulting from expectations) you have made about their behavior, and how have these translated into judgments about who they are as a person(s)?

8. Have you experienced serious trauma or abuse by a close friend or relative as a child? Have you received some healing? What still needs to happen to get closer to where you think God may want to take you in the healing process?

9. What anxieties do you have about memories of your past?

10. Healing is a journey. Explain.

11. Which area from your childhood needs the most mending (e.g., trust, play, relationships, fear, emotions, faith, etc.)? Explain.

12. Anger, hate, and rage do not "just happen." Jesus points this out in Matthew 5:21-22.
"You have heard that it was said to the people long ago, 'Do not murder,[a] and anyone who murders will be subject to judgment.' But I tell you that anyone who is angry with his brother[b] will be subject to judgment. Again, anyone who says to his brother, 'Raca' is answerable to the Sanhedrin. But anyone who says, 'You fool!' will be in danger of the fire of hell." Also read in context.

Explain how "critical judgments" are at the root of what Christ is teaching in these verses.

Session Seven — Forgiveness and Reconciliation

Beginning Part Three — Conflict Resolution:
An Interpersonal Matter Between God, Man, and Fellowman

Read the Following:
Chapter 7 — Forgiveness and Reconciliation
Follow–up and Practice for Part Three – Conflict Resolution

Some Key Points:

1. Forgiveness and reconciliation are inevitable experiences in worthwhile interpersonal relationships, stirred by conflict and testing of character in an irreparably (humanly speaking) broken world.

2. Love, as defined by God, is what our relationships with people should be based on. God's love for us is the model.

3. Forgiveness must not be confused with reconciliation. "Forgiveness is about *me*; reconciliation is about *us*."

4. In the similar manner that repentance and confession are keys in reconciling oneself to God, repentance and confession are crucial in reconciliation with fellowman.

Session Seven Reflection and Discussion Questions

Escaping the Pain of Offense

1. Meditate on Jeremiah 2:13 and surrounding verses. Write down your interpretation.

2. How hard is it for you to say "I was wrong?" What blessings have you missed out of by being "non–teachable" in this regard?

3. What was your picture of God in your growing up years? How has it changed and how do you see God now?

4. On a scale of 1 to 10 (1 being never; 10 being always); Can God be trusted? What would it take for God to be trusted one notch higher (e.g. if 5, what would make it 6) Are you trusting Christ to remove your dysfunction (sin), or are you relying on your own willpower to change? Explain.

5. We draw near to God in order to know his desires for us and to know how we can please him. Explain how you are drawing near to God (e.g., through devotions, worship, prayer, fellowship, journaling, meditations, etc.).

6. In your relationship with _____(problem person), have you made assumptions about them that are incorrect; ungodly; unhealthy for them or for you? Explain the source and what you can do to get free.

7. Looking back on some of the most fruitful relationships in your life, how has conflict (differences or disagreements) worked for the good? List and explain.

8. Explain your thoughts about 1 John 4:19-21. "We love because he first loved us. If anyone says, "I love God," yet

hates his brother, he is a liar. For anyone who does not love his brother, whom he has seen, cannot love God, whom he has not seen. And he has given us this command: Whoever loves God must also love his brother."

9. The Cycle of Offense described in Chapter 1, states that we become an offender (to keep the cycle going). We sometimes offend other people (or even ourselves), but our *greatest* offense is against God. Explain how 1 John 4:19-21 confirms that offending God is our *greatest* problem; even bigger than offending people.

Session Eight — Reconciliation in Relationships

Read the Following:
Chapter 8 — Reconciliation in Relationships
Follow-up and Practice for Part Three – Conflict Resolution

Some Key Points:

1. Our hearts are the wellsprings of all our thoughts, desires, words, and actions. Therefore, it is also the source of our conflicts. Bible passages presented here describe the root cause of conflict, which is unmet desires in our hearts.

2. Family and intergenerational transmission of sin is a major source of root issues. This does not preclude personal responsibility for each person to examine him or herself and allow God to extract the bad roots.

3. Marriage, Church, and Community all present unique challenges and opportunities to practice forgiveness and reconciliation.

4. Culture plays a key role in maturity of relationship. Acknowledgement and ownership of values and beliefs makes the way for genuine communication to occur. On both ends of sending and receiving a message, values and beliefs impact interpretation of verbal and nonverbal interactions. The same honesty and humility discussed earlier as it applies to individuals taking responsibility for their own part of an offense, is applicable in a cultural context as well.

STUDY GUIDE

Session Eight Reflection and Discussion Questions

1. Explain how your religious (Church) experience may have reinforced your tendency to deny your need for healing. When people cannot be transparent, how does it affect the Body of Christ?

2. What particular character/behavior traits (both positive and negative) have been present in your family line? How have these affected your life to this point?

3. Are there any "family secrets" that you are aware of that others are not, or that you feel are being withheld from your knowledge? Explain. Examine the hurt and ask God if He would have you play any role in healing. (Caution: be careful and KNOW it is God before you act on anything!)

4. Have you wrongly "judged" one or both of your parents; grandparents; sibling(s)? What might you still be "reaping" from these judgments, and what does God want you to do about it?

5. On a scale of 1 to 10 (1 being never and 10 being always) how easy do you think it is for you to discern a cultural difference when you are trying to communicate with someone but neither of you seems to be getting through? Explain your answer.

6. Do you regularly hang out with people of different race, ethnicity, social status etc.? Why, or why not? Is there a particular group of people you fear getting to know, more than others? Why? What would it take to overcome your separation from another people group(s)?

7. Have you witnessed prejudice in any way from anyone/group? Describe your feelings. How can you be part of the solution instead of perpetuating the problem?

8. How have "cultural" (people group) assumptions and faulty thinking in regards to "culture" impacted your life? What culture(s)?

9. Try to identify some "strong holds" in your thinking patterns that hinder relating to other people in a godly manner. What is the source and what judgments may be attached to these?

10. Are you a good listener? Do you know someone who is a good listener? What makes this person a good listener, and in general, what defines a good listener? What can you change to become a better listener?

11. Are you aware of the personality differences between you and your closest friend(s)? What are these differences, and what difference do they make on your outlook on life? How do they factor in your interpretation of your friend's actions, and your friend's interpretation of your actions?

12. How could you become a better communicator? What would your friend(s) say would make you a better communicator?

13. Recall a supportive/mentor relationship you've had in the past. Describe at least one important aspect of that relationship experience.

14. How might the victim/predator cycle described in Part One apply to the discussion of inter-group tensions regarding perceived rights of a group (discussion in Chapter Eight section called Cultural Unforgiveness)?

Session Nine — Conclusions Part I

Read the Following:
Chapter 9 — Conclusion – Part I
Follow-up and Practice for Part Three – Conflict Resolution

Some Key Points:

1. Four key themes guide the content of this book. The first is the redemptive plan of God; second, the centrality of Jesus Christ; third, practicing the elements of forgiveness; and four, paving the way for reconciliation and conflict resolution.

2. Every aspect of forgiveness is focused on God and His love.

3. The Church, as a diverse family of God's people and as a community centered in God's love, must learn to allow cultural and theological differences to unite rather than divide.

4. Forgiveness involves three main components: the Gift, the choice, and the fruit (i.e. Jesus as God's Gift of love, our choice to surrender, and the human experience that follows).

Session Nine Reflection and Discussion Questions

1. What are some important things to keep in mind when helping another person pray through their inner struggles?

2. Using the life song repertoire analogy discussed at the end of Chapter Eight, explain how practicing forgiveness demonstrates a life growing in Christ-likeness. How might this become a "cultural" phenomena in a Christian's personal relationship with God?

3. Is forgiveness a) a gift, b) a choice, c) an emotion, d) all of the above? If the answer is d: all of these three elements, explain why you would agree or disagree.

4. For the Christian, is forgiveness an "option"? Resolve your answer with 1 John 4:19-20.

5. Explain how the practice of forgiveness and reconciliation witnesses Christ's love to the world.

6. Drawing from your experience, how could the Church (in America) demonstrate better practices of respecting and honoring people of diverse backgrounds and cultures? What evidence/examples of this respect have you already witnessed?

Review or revisit any unanswered questions from previous sessions.

Session Ten — Conclusions Part II

Read the Following:

Chapter 9 — Conclusion – Part II

Follow-up and Practice for Part Three – Conflict Resolution

Appendix A – Resources and sample prayers

Appendix B – Author's Personal Story and Healing Journey

Appendix C – Overcoming an Abortion

Some Key Points:

1. Continue unfinished points from Session Nine

2. The Appendices in the book *Escaping the Pain of Offense* contain some resources to help work through specific issues on the healing journey.

3. Make this as personal as possible to apply what you have learned and to allow God to continue to change your heart towards the goal of closer fellowship with Him and other people.

4. If some of the questions in the Study are too difficult or too probing, return to the material sometime within a year. An increased awareness and practice of these themes can help measure your spiritual growth. Refer to Appendix B for more on the author's personal story of healing. You may want to seek a Christian counselor to help further process through a place you become stuck.

Session Ten Reflection and Discussion Questions

1. Which of the resources (in the Appendices) have you found most helpful and why?

2. Reflecting back over the entire study, what part(s) have impacted you the most? Explain.

3. How has this study changed your life (as compared to before reading the book)?

    a. In what ways is your understanding and practice of forgiveness different?

    b. What fruit is evident in your relationship with God and others, and how you view yourself?

4. What area(s) do you need to review and revisit? Why? When will you do this?

5. Are you ready to seek the help of a trusted friend or counselor to process further or obtain their perspective on your progress?

6. Do you need to see a doctor to rule out a medical explanation for problems you are experiencing?

7. Are you trusting the God of the Bible as your "primary physician"?

    a. Is Father God the primary One in whom you find your identity, protection, and provision?

    b. Is Jesus your primary source of companionship and communication?

    c. Is the Holy Spirit your Chief comforter, nurturer, and teacher?

Review or revisit any unanswered questions from previous sessions.

About the Author

Edward and his wife Stephanie, married since 1980, are parents of four adult children and are active in community service and church ministry. They are Innkeepers at Blue Rock Bed and Breakfast near Lancaster, PA hosting many who come to their location for vacation, respite, and healing ministry. See more at http://bluerockbnb.com. For ministry information see http://healing.bluerockbnb.com.

Dr. Hersh completed a Doctor of Religious Studies program in Conflict Management at Trinity Theological Seminary in Newburgh, IN and earned a Master of Arts in Human Service Counseling from Regent University in Virginia Beach, VA. Pastor Ed has completed advanced level training in techniques for healing of the inner person.As an ordained minister he provides chaplain services and pastoral counseling to individuals and families. His writing, teaching, and training ministry have taken him to foreign lands including Europe and southeast Asia. He maintains membership in American Association of Christian Counselors (AACC), Christian Association of Psychological Studies (CAPS), HarvestNet Inc., Lord's House of Prayer, and other professional and ministry organizations. Past experiences in employment have included seventeen years in software development and a variety of jobs in foreign language teaching, social services, and adaptive technology training. Ed's volunteer Board service has included the Susquehanna Association for the Blind and Vision Impaired, Bethany Christian Services, Virginia Beach Mayor's Committee on Persons with Disabilities Breath of Life Ministries, and Pennsylvania Council of the Blind. Ed and Stephanie co-founded a group called Respect Young America (advocating for teens and pre-born children), and Ed is the founding President of Red Rose Council of the Blind.

Since transitioning to pastoral and counseling ministry in 2000, Ed has worked with a number of churches and ministries including Light of Hope Community Service Organization in Lancaster. Dr. Hersh's desire is to see professional and para-professional services connected for mental health and addictions treatment to care for the whole person—spirit, mind, and body.

Lancaster County Pennsylvania is a popular tourist destination and has many attractions to make a wonderful family vacation. They would welcome your stay at the Blue Rock Bed and Breakfast. They also host small retreats and in addition to the hospitality and prayer counseling they offer training to help leaders and lay counseling teams sharpen their skills in prayer counseling and healing ministry.

Read more about the author's personal healing journey in Appendix B of the book.

Visit the author's blog at: http://authoredhersh.blogspot.com.

ENDNOTES for PART ONE

Chapter One

1.   John 3:16.

Chapter Two

1.   McDowell 2002.

2.   Barna 2006.

3.   Sandford 1999; Kurath 2003; DeMoss 2005, p. 24.

4.   Barna 2007.

5.   Barna 2006.

6.   Barna 2001.

7.   Jeffress 2000, pp. 210-211.

8.   Jeffress 2000, p. 225.

9.   Cunningham 1985, p. 141.

10.   Hargrave 1999; McCullough, Pargament, & Thoresen 2000; Worthington 1998.

11.   Enright & North 1998; Worthington 1998.

12.   Hersh 2010.

Chapter Three and Follow-up for Part One

1.   Gen. 3:7-9.

2.   Augsburger 1996.

3.   Luke 24:27.

4.   1 John 4:10.

5.   Boice 1986.

6.   Gen. 1:27.

7.   Gen. 2:7.

8.   Isa. 64:8; Ps. 139.

9.   Isa. 43:7.

10.   Ps. 139:13-14; Rom. 5:8; Eph. 2:10.

11.   Gen. 3:1-7.

12.   Job 1:7ff; John 12:31; 14:30; Eph. 2:2.

13.   Ps. 51:5; Rom. 7:18; Tit. 1:15.

14.   Gen. 3:7.

15.   Gen. 3:12.

16.   Gen. 3:13.

17.   Isa. 64:5b-7; Jer. 17:9.

18.   Eph. 2:4.

19.   Rom. 5:8-9.

20.   Eph. 2:8.

21.   Morris 1981.

22.   John 3:16.

23.   Gen. 3:21.

24.   2 Cor. 3:18; Col. 3:10; Boice 1986; Grudem 1994.

25.   Eph. 4:32; cf. Col. 3:13.

26.   Eph. 2:4; Ps. 106:8.

27.   Rev. 19:7-8.

28.   Eph. 5:25-33.

29.   MacArthur 1998; Sande 2004; Kendall 2007.

30.   1 Cor. 15:54-57.

31.   See MacArthur 1998, Appendix One, for a more thorough explanation of the doctrine of the atonement.

32.   MacArthur 1998, p. 12.

33.   Rom. 5:10; 8:7.

34.   Ps. 5:5.

35.   Ps. 58:3; Adams 1973.

36.   Eph. 2:1, 3:12.

37.   James 2:10.

38.   Rom. 3:10-18.

39.   John 3:16.

40.   Rom. 4:5, 7, 8.

41. Rom. 3:25-26.

42. Sandford 1982; Augsberger 1988; Sande 2004; Kendall 2007.

43. Jeffress 2000.

44. Rom. 3:26.

45. Ps. 85:10.

46. 2 Cor. 5:18.

47. MacArthur 1998; Kurath 2003.

48. Rom. 8:7-8.

49. MacArthur 1998, p. 17.

50. Gen. 3:9.

51. Jer. 13:15-17.

52. Hos. 3:1-3.

53. MacArthur 1998, pp. 18-19.

54. MacArthur 1998, p. 21.

55. 1 Pet. 2:24.

56. Rom. 3:25; Heb. 2:17; 1 John 2:2; 4:10.

57. Swedes 1984; Miller 1994; MacArthur 1998; Seaman's 2003.

58. MacArthur 1998, p. 26.

59. Miller 1994; MacArthur 1998; Worthington 2005; Kendall 2007.

60. cf. Gen. 15:6 with Gen. 17:10.

61. Frost 2005.

62. Morris 1981, p. 131.

63. 1 John 4:8.

64. David (Ps. 51:11), Jesus (Acts 10:38), the early church (Acts 1:8), and all believers (Rom. 15:13).

65. Rom. 5:5.

66. Piper 1979.

67. 1 Cor. 13:4-7.

68. Piper 1979.

69. Heb. 10:22.

70. John 3:16.
71. Isa. 66:1-4; Matt. 18:21-35.
72. Matt. 18:28.

ENDNOTES for PART TWO

Chapter Four

1. John 1:12, 3:16; Rom. 3:22; 1 Tim. 4:10.
2. Grudem 1994, p. 747.
3. Phil. 2:12.
4. Grudem 1994, p. 747.
5. Ibid., p. 746.
6. See Tit. 3:5; 1 John 3:9; 1 Cor. 6:11; Acts 20:32.
7. See Rom. 6:11-18.
8. Rom. 6:18.
9. Rom. 6:11.
10. Rom. 6:12-13.
11. Rom. 6:19.
12. 2 Cor. 3:18.
13. Rom. 6:12-13; 1 John 1:8.
14. See Heb. 12:23; Grudem 1994, p. 747.
15. Grudem 1994, p. 753.
16. Heb. 12:5-11; Phil. 2:13; Heb. 13:20-21; 1 Cor. 1:30.
17. Heb. 12:2; 1 Pet. 2:21; 1 John 2:6.
18. 1 Pet. 1:2; 2 Thess. 2:13; Gal. 5:216-18, 22, 23; cf. Rom. 8:14.
19. Grudem 1994, p. 755.
20. Jeffress 2000, p. 10.
21. Hallowell 2004; Worthington 2004.
22. Matt. 22:36-40.
23. Powlison 1995; Friesen 1998, p. 80; Seamans 2003, p. 78.
24. Baars 2003, p. 30.

25. Hersh & Hughes 2005.
26. Ibid.
27. Col. 2:2; 1 John 4:16; Augsburger 1988, p. 15.
28. Rom. 12:1-2.
29. John 3:2-6; 1 Pet. 1:23.
30. Frost 2005, p. 17.
31. John 8:28, 14:23, 31; 2 Pet. 1:17.
32. John 8:28.
33. Phil. 2:7.
34. Matt. 4:1-11.
35. Matt. 26:56; John 1:11, 7:1-5, 13:21-30; Luke 4:14-30, 22:5.
36. John 4:6-8, 31, 32.
37. John 11:33, 35, 36.
38. John 12:27; Luke 22:39-46; Hersh & Hughes 2005.
39. Matt. 26:37-68; 27:26-32.
40. Matt. 27:46; 2 Cor. 5:21.
41. Rom. 3:17.
42. Matt. 26:28.
43. Luke 4:18-21.
44. Dial 1999.
45. Rom. 8:28, 18-26.
46. Gen. 2:7, King James Version.
47. See also Job 10:12; Ezek. 37:14; John 6:63; Rom. 8:6; 1 Cor. 15:45; 2 Cor. 3:16; Gal. 6:9; Rev. 22:17.
48. Augsburger 1988; Kurath 2003; Worthington 2004.
49. Baars 2003.
50. For example: Deut. 11:18; 1 Sam. 2:35; Job 38:36; Ps. 7:9, 26:2, 64:6, 73:2; Isa. 46:8; Jer. 11:20, 17:10, 20:12, 23:26, 31:33; Matt. 22:37; Mark 12:30; Luke 10:27; Acts 4:32; Phil. 4:7; Heb. 8:10, 10:16; Rev. 2:23.

51. Augsburger 1988, p. 63.
52. Heb. 10:1-25; see the discussion in the previous chapter.
53. Heb. 10:14.
54. Mark 7:6a.
55. Augsburger 1988; Grudem 1994, p. 756-757; Baars 2003; Worthington 2004.
56. Lloyd-Jones 1965, p. 52.
57. Matt. 22:37; Friesen et.al. 2004.
58. Baars 2003; Kurath 2003, pp. 62-65.
59. Grudem 1994, pp. 472-489.
60. Prov. 13:16; 14:8; 15:14
61. Ps. 51:6.
62. Heb. 10:22; Sandford 1982; Jeffress 2000; Fosarelli 2002; Kurath 2003; Friesen et.al. 2004; Sande 2004; Worthington 2004.
63. Jer. 17:9.
64. See Eph. 4:18; Sandford 1982; Fosarelli 2002; Friesen et.al. 2004.
65. Sandford 1982, 22-27; Kurath 2003.
66. Grudem 1994, p. 747.
67. Rom. 7:15.
68. 2 Cor. 3:18.
69. Ps. 1:1-3; 40:4; John 13:17; James 1:25; Kurath 2003.
70. 1 Thess. 1:10.
71. Shogren 1993.
72. Bultmann 1955, Part IV, pp. 203-204.
73. Adams 1994; Powlison 1995.
74. Isa. 66:2.
75. John 14:23.
76. Worthington 2004, pp. 143-145.

77.   Isa. 64:6.

78.   Sandford 1982, p. 41.

79.   1 Cor. 3:11-13.

80.   Rom. 4; Gal. 2:21.

81.   Gen. 3:6-11.

82.   John 3:16; Rev. 22:17.

83.   Kendall 2007.

84.   Jeffress 2000, pp. 51-52.

85.   Hersh & Hughes 2005.

86.   Holmgren 1993; Jeffress 2000.

87.   Jeffress 2003; Stortz 2007.

88.   Rom. 3:23.

89.   Jeffress 2000, p. 66.

90.   Sande 2004; Worthington 2004.

91.   DeMoss 2006, pp. 169-170.

92.   Ibid., p. 170.

93.   Ibid., p. 171.

94.   Ibid., pp. 170-176.

95.   2 Cor. 1:3-4.

Chapter Five

1.   Miller 1994, 40; Kendall 2007, p. 68.

2.   Rom. 15:7.

3.   Matt. 6:14-15.

4.   Sandford 1982; Miller 1994; Kurath 2003; Kendall 2007.

5.   Sandford 1999, p. 61.

6.   Matt. 18:22-23.

7.   2 Cor. 3:18, 4:6; Heb. 13:21.

8.   Isa. 29:16.

9.   DeMoss 2006, p. 150.

10. Smedes 1996.
11. Ps. 139:34.
12. 2 Cor. 5:7.
13. 1 Cor. 8.
14. Rom. 14:5b; Miller 1994, p. 205.
15. Smedes 1996, p. 29; Jeffress 2000, p. 110; Enright 2001, p. 263; Sande 2004; Worthington 2004, p. 221.
16. Miller 1994.
17. Ibid.
18. Enright 2001; Worthington 2004; Omunga 2005, p. 18.
19. Luke 4:18; Isa. 61:1.
20. Karath 2003, p. 61.
21. Ibid., p. 333.
22. Heb. 12:10-11.
23. Kurath 2003, p. 52.
24. Matt. 25:32-34.
25. Matt. 18:17.
26. Prov. 10:13.
27. Matt. 7:1-2; Kurath 2003.
28. Heb. 12:15.
29. Ps. 42:6; 43:5.
30. Worthington 2005, p. 188.
31. Matt. 7:3.
32. Sandford 1999, p. 75.
33. Augsburger 1988; Miller 1994; Smedes 1996; Sandford 1999; Enright 2001; Hallowell 2004; Worthington 2004; Kendall 2007.
34. Sandford 1999, p. 68.
35. Heb. 11:6.
36. Augsburger 1988, p. 35; see James 1:13-15.

37. James 1:16-20.
38. Grudem 1994, pp. 756-757.
39. Col. 3:10.
40. Phil. 1:9.
41. Rom. 12:2.
42. Col. 1:10; 2 Cor. 10:5.
43. Grudem 1994, p. 756.
44. Rom. 6:17.
45. Eph. 4:31.
46. Phil. 2:13.
47. 2 Cor. 7:1.
48. 1 Cor. 7:34.
49. 1 Thess. 5:23.
50. 2 Cor. 7:1; cf. 1 Cor. 7:34.
51. 1 Cor. 9:27.
52. Rom. 6:12.
53. 1 Cor. 6:13.
54. Grudem 1994, p. 757.
55. 2 Cor. 4:16.
56. Gen. 2:27; Eccles. 12:7; Ps. 31:9; Matt. 10:28.
57. Hodge 1997, p. 45; Cooper 2000, p. 204; Hoekema 1986, p. 217.
58. Scazzero 2006.
59. Ps. 35; 42; 57; 62; 69; 103; 119.
60. Smedes 1996; Fountain 1999; Enright 2001; Witvliet 2001; Seamands 2003; Edmondson 2004; Friesen et.al. 2004; Hallowell 2004; Sande 2004; Worthington 2004; DeMoss 2006, p. 46.
61. Hallowell 2004.
62. Ibid.

63. Sandford 1982; Lane & Tripp 2006.

64. Gal. 5:22-23.

65. Gal. 5:19-21.

66. Enright 2001; Baars 2003; Hallowell 2004; Worthington 2004.

67. Fountain 1999.

68. Ibid.

69. Seyle & Fortier 1950.

70. Fountain 1999; Baars 2003; Hallowell 2004; Worthington 2004; Edmondson 2004.

71. Fountain 1999.

72. 1 Thess. 5:23-24.

73. Fountain 1999.

74. Matt. 9:35; Acts 10:36-38.

75. Liu 1999.

76. Luke 17:19.

77. Seamands 2003, p. 132.

78. Luke 23:24.

79. Matt. 10:1.

80. Matt. 28:19-20.

81. John 20:22-23.

82. Seamands 2003.

Chapter Six and Follow-up for Part Two

1. Storti 1999.

2. Matt. 7:1-5.

3. Kendall 2007.

4. Ibid., p. 98.

5. Sandford 1982; Kendall 2007.

6. Matt. 7:3.

7. Sande 2004; Kendall 2007.

8. Kendall 2007, p. 111.
9. Matt. 7:5.
10. Grudem 1994.
11. Erickson 1985.
12. Grudem 1994, p. 746.
13. Ibid.. 1994.
14. John 3:16.
15. Fosarelli 2002; Friesen et.al. 2004; Worthington 2004.
16. Smedes 1996.
17. Rom. 12:1.
18. Smedes 1996, p. 7.
19. Miller 1994; Sandford 1999; Sande 2002, 2004; Braybrooke 2003; Ruth 2007.
20. Kurath 2003; Day 2008.
21. See Luke 8:39; John 9:25, 30-33; Acts 5:41-42.
22. Rev. 21:3-5.
23. Sandford 1999; Seamands 2003.
24. Eccles. 1:18.
25. Prov. 20:5.
26. Eph. 3:10-12; James 1:2-4.
27. Friesen et.al. 2004, p. 15.
28. Smedes 1996; Enright 2001; Seamands 2003; Friesen et.al. 2004; Hallowell 2004; Sande 2004; Worthington 2004; Kendall 2007.
29. 2 Cor. 12:10.
30. e.g., Ps. 10:14.
31. 2 Cor. 12:9.
32. Rom. 8:28.
33. Friesen et.al. 2004, p. 16.
34. James 1:8.

35. Hersh & Hughes 2005.

36. Friesen 2004, p. 17.

37. James 1:4.

38. Eph. 4:26, 27.

39. Mathias 2002, p. 114.

40. Heb. 12:15.

41. Rom. 3:10-18.

42. Heb. 12:15, NASB.

43. Sandford 1999, p. 108.

44. Mark 4:20.

45. Sandford 1999.

46. Sandford 1982/1999; Fosarelli 2002; Friesen et.al. 2004; Frost 2005.

47. Prov. 22:6.

48. Sandford 1982/1999.

49. Isa. 6:9-10; Mark 4:12.

50. Adams 1973, p. 172.

51. Prov. 20:5.

52. Sandford 1999; Kylstra 2003; Frost 2005.

53. 2 Cor. 10:4, 5, KJV.

54. MacArthur 1998; Cheong 2005.

55. Rom. 5:5.

56. Phil. 2:12-13.

57. John 3:16-17.

58. Frost 2005.

59. Eph. 1:14.

60. 2 Cor. 5:18.

61. Rom. 12:3.

62. Matt. 22:37; Mark 12:30; Luke 10:27.

63. Eccles. 11:9.

64.   Jeffress 2000, p. 27.

65.   Kurath 2003.

66.   See Luke 6:43-45.

67.   Kurath 2003, p. 50.

68.   Gen. 3:22-23.

69.   Heb. 12:15.

70.   Edmondson 2004; Sande 2004; Worthington 2004; Sandford 1999.

71.   Sandford 1999; Sande 2004.

72.   Sandford 1999; Enright 2001; Seamands 2003; Sande 2004; Worthington 2004.

73.   Ezek. 14:3; 1 John 5:21; Anderson 1993; Sande 2002; Kylstra 2003; Powlison 2003; Frost 2005; DeMoss 2006.

74.   Lane & Tripp, 2006.

75.   Worthington 2005, p. 75.

76.   1 Cor. 2:11.

77.   Isa. 30:15.

78.   Matt. 11:11-15.

79. Matt. 11:28-30.

ENDNOTES for PART THREE

Chapter Seven

1.   Worthingon 2004, p. 35.

2.   Matt. 7:1-5.

3.   Augsburger 1988; MacArthur 1998; Sandford 1999; Jeffress 2000; Kurath 2003; Seamands 2003; Sande 2004; DeMoss 2006.

4.   Sande 2004, p. 20.

5.   See Josh. 22:10-34.

6.   See Acts 15:39; 1 Cor. 12:12-31.

Endnotes

7. See Gen. 13:1-12.

8. See James 4:1-2.

9. Matt. 5:21-22.

10. Matt. 5:23-24.

11. Hansen 1979, p. 93.

12. 1 John 4:19-21.

13. 1 John 4:19-21.

14. Sande 2004, p. 59; Kraybill 2007, p. 100.

15. Sandford 1982; MacArthur 1998; Sande 2004.

16. Exod. 4:10-12; Job 1:6-12; 42:11; Ps.71:20-22; Isa. 45:5-7; Lam. 3:37-38; Amos 3-6; 1 Pet. 3:17.

17. Sande 2004, p. 62.

18. 1 Cor. 13:5.

19. John 17:5; Piper 2003.

20. Tit. 2:14.

21. Col. 3:1; Powlison 1995.

22. Cheong 2005.

23. Isa. 61:3.

24. 1 John 4:12; 1 Cor. 13:6; Kierkegaard 1847/1995.

25. Kierkegaard 1847/1995.

26. Burnaby 1938.

27. Col. 2:2.

28. Burnaby 1938, p. 177.

29. Morris 1981.

30. Eph. 4:16.

31. Kierkegaard 1847/1995, p. 215.

32. Cheong 2005.

33. Augsburger 1988; Cheong 2005.

34. Mark 12:29-31.

35. MacArthur 1998; Sandford 1999, p. 83; Seamands 2003.

254

36. Jer. 15:15-17.
37. Sandford 1999.
38. Ps. 24:3-4.
39. Luke 22:42.
40. 2 Cor. 5:21.
41. Sandford 1999, p. 83.
42. Augsburger 1988; Sandford 1999; Enright 2001; Worthington 2004; Kendall 2007.
43. Jeffress 2000, p. 110.
44. Smedes 1996, p. 25; Enright 2001, p. 263; Sande 2004, p. 219; Worthington 2004, p. 221
45. Smedes 1996, p. 35.
46. Sande 2004, p. 219.
47. Matt. 5:24; cf. 1 Cor. 7:11; 2 Cor. 5:18-20.
48. Worthington 2004, p. 219.
49. Enright 2001, p. 31; Worthington 2004.
50. Luke 17:3-4.
51. Augsburger 1988; Miller 1994; MacArthur 1998; Jeffress 2000; Hallowell 2004; Sande 2004; Worthington 2004; Kendall 2007.
52. Sande 2004.
53. Worthington 2004, p. 221.
54. 2 Cor. 5:18.
55. Sandford 1982; Adams 1994, p. 95.
56. Deut. 1:42ff.
57. Isa. 55:9.
58. Isa. 55:10-11.
59. Adams 1994.
60. Ibid.
61. Num. 5:7.

62.   Luke 19:8.

63.   Sande 2004, p. 276.

64.   see Ps. 119:67, 71; Prov. 19:19.

65.   Matt. 18:22-27.

66.   Luke 19:8-9; Augsburger 1988; Holmgren 1993; Miller 1994; MacArthur 1998, 188; Jeffress 2000, 118; Hallowell 2004; Sande 2004, 278; Worthington 2004.

Chapter Eight

1.   Sandford 1999; Rye 2002; Friesen 2004; Sande 2004; DeMoss 2006.

2.   James 4:1-3.

3.   Mark 7:20-23.

4.   Luke 12:13-15.

5.   Sande 2004, p. 114.

6.   Sandford 1999, p. 100.

7.   Sande 2002; Kylstra 2003.

8.   Gen. 50:24; Exod. 3:16; Matt. 22:32; Acts 3:13.

9.   Ps. 139.

10.   Heb. 7:9-10.

11.   Gen. 3.

12.   Sandford 1982; Hargrave 1994; Kylstra 2003, p. 104; Worthington 2004.

13.   Kylstra 2003.

14.   Sandford 1982; Hargrave 1994; Kylstra 2003.

15.   Exod. 20:4-6.

16.   Kylstra 2003.

17.   Powlison 2005.

18.   MacArthur 1993; Sandford 1999; Sande 2002,2004; Kylstra 2003; Seamans 2003.

19. Kylstra 2003, p. 113.

20. Jer. 17:9-10.

21. Friesen 1998; Shore 2007.

22. Lev. 26:40-42.

23. Richards 2005.

24. Lane & Tripp 2006.

25. Sande 2002.

26. Eph. 5:31.

27. Eph. 5:25.

28. Prov. 22:6; Worthington 2004; Newheiser 2005.

29. MacArthur 1998, p. 178.

30. Gen. 3:17-18.

31. Rom. 3:19-21; Eph. 3:10-11; Phil. 2:12.

32. Ps. 133:1-3.

33. Sandford 1999, 160; Sande 2004.

34. Rom. 7:21-25.

35. 1 Cor. 3:2-3, 13:11-12; Eph. 4:2-3.

36. Heb. 12:15; Rom. 2:1.

37. Matt. 18:23-35.

38. Prov. 20:30; 25:11; 27:5; 2 Cor. 4:16-18; 1 John 4:17.

39. 2 Cor. 2:5-11; Eph. 4:26-27, 31-32.

40. Luke 11:39-40; 1 John 4:19-20.

41. Matt. 11:28.

42. Rev. 22:17.

43. Sandford 1999, Sande 2004; DeMoss 2006, p. 174.

44. John 20:21-23.

45. Matt. 11:28-29.

46. Isa. 30:15.

47. Sande 2004; Worthington 2004.

48. Sande 2002, p. 162.

49. John 4:7-26.

50. Luke 19:1-10; John 8:10-11.

51. Sande 2004, p. 160.

52. Matt. 18:15-17.

53. Matt. 18:22-35.

54. Ps. 32:5; 41:4.

55. Sande 2004, p. 127.

56. Luke 19:8; Acts 19:18.

57. Sandford 1982; Sande 2004.

58. Smedes 1984, 60; Smedes 1996, p. 14.

59. DeMoss 2006, p. 71.

60. Perkins & Rice 2000.

61. Storti 1999, p. 5.

62. Ibid.

63. Sande 2004.

64. Eph. 4:7-13.

65. 1 Cor. 12:12-31.

66. Rom. 14:1.

67. Sande 2004, p. 53.

68. Eph. 4:29-31.

69. Eph. 4:32.

70. 1 Cor. 12:21-31.

71. Sandford 1999; Sande 2004, p. 49; Richards 2005, p. 197.

72. Eph. 4:1-13.

73. Rom. 15:7; cf. 14:1-13.

74. Gal. 6:10; Rom. 12:18.

75. Worthington 2004, p. 256.

76. Ibid.

77. Storti 1999; Worthington 2004.

78. Worthington 2004, p. 257.

79. Ibid.

80. Ibid.

81. Adams 1994; Miller 1994; Storti 1999; Enright 2001; Sande 2004; Worthington 2004; Kraybill 2007; Ruth 2007.

82. Worthington 2004, p. 257.

83. Sande 2002, 2004.

84. Sande 2004; Worthington 2004.

85. Fields 2005.

86. Powilson 1995; Kraybill et.al. 2007, p. 146.

87. Kraybill, Nolt & Weaver-Zercher 2007, p. 51.

88. Kraybill et.al. 2007; Ruth 2007.

89. Ibid.

90. van Bragt 1968.

91. Kraybill, Nolt & Weaver-Zercher 2007, p. 28.

92. Storti 1999; Kraybill et.al. 2007.

93. Ruth 2007, p. 146.

94. Ezek. 36:26.

95. John 1:14; 2 Cor. 3:3.

Chapter Nine and Follow-up for Part Three

1. Ezek. 18:4; 2 Pet. 2:8.

2. Gen. 1:27.

3. Phil. 1:6; 2:13; 1 John 4:12.

4. 2 Cor. 10:3-5.

5. Cunningham 1985; Murphy & Hampton 1988; Sandford 1999; Enright 2000/2001; Worthington 2001/2003; Shults & Sandage 2003.

6. 1 Cor. 13:6.

7. Eccles. 1:18; Edwards 1852/2000.

8. Sandford 1982, 1999; Grudem 1994; Jeffress 2000; Seamands 2003; Friesen 2004.

9. Gal. 5:22-23.

10. MacArthur 1998, p. 92.

11. Gal. 2:20-21; 6:14; Eph. 3:11; 1 Pet. 1:2, 3:18; Heb. 9:15.

12. Eph. 2:8-10.

13. Cunningham 1985; Adams 1989; Miller 1994; DiBlasio 2000; MacArthur 1998; Sandford 1999; Enright 2000; Worthington 2003; Sande 2004; DeMoss 2006.

14. Hong 1984; Jones 1995; Pargament & Rye 1998; Sandford 1999; Sande 2004; Kraybill et.al. 2007.

15. Miller 1994, p. 176.

16. 1 Thess. 5:23.

17. Rom. 8:28.

18. Matt. 10:37-39.

19. Edwards 1852/2000; Kierkegaard 1847/1995; Morris 1981.

20. Phil. 3:10; Enright & Fitzgibbons 2000.

21. Sandford 1982; Augsburger 1988; Hampton 1988; Hargrave 1994; Jones 1995; Kierkegaard 1847/1995; Sande 2002/2004; Worthington 2003.

22. Jones 1995; Piper 1979.

23. Hong 1984; Jones 1995.

24. 1 Cor. 12:12-31.

25. Rom. 14:1; Sande 2004, p. 53.

26. 2 Cor. 5:16-21.

27. John 3:16.

28. Luke 19:10.

29. John 20:19-23.

30. Acts 1:8.

31. Matt. 6:12.

32. 2 Cor. 1:3-7.
33. Cox 2008.
34. Jeffress 2000.
35. Smedes 1984; Smedes 1996.
36. Lev. 19:17, 18; Rom. 5:8.
37. Smedes 1984, p. 22.
38. Ibid. 1984, p. 23.
39. 1 John 4:19-20.
40. Enright 2001; Worthington 2004.
41. Sandford 1999, 85; Stortz 2007.
42. Sandford 1982/1999; Hargrave 1994; Kylstra 2003.
43. Sandford 1999, p. 111.
44. Ps. 46.
45. Isa. 30:15.

Bibliography

Abbott, D.A., M.M. Berry, and W.H. Meredith. Religious belief and practice: A potential asset in helping families. Family Relations: *Journal of Applied Family and Child Studies*, 39 (1990): 443-448.

Adams, Jay. *The Christian counselor's manual.* Philippianslipsburg, NJ: Presbyterian and Reformed Publishing Co., 1973.

_____. *From forgiven to forgiving.* Amityville, NY: Calvary Press, 1994.

Aiken, L.S. and S.G. West. *Multiple regression: Testing and interpreting interactions.* Newbury Park, CA: Sage Publications, 1991.

Anderson, N.T. *The bondage breaker.* Eugene, OR: Harvest House Publishers, 993.

Anderson, W.T. and T.D. Hargrave. Contextual family therapy and older people: Building trust in the intergenerational family. *Journal of Family Therapy, 3* (1990): 311-320.

Augsburger, David. *The freedom of forgiveness: seventy times seven.* Revelation and expanded. Chicago IL: Moody Press, 1988.

Baars, C. *Feeling and healing your emotions.* Orlando, FL: Bridge-Logos, 2003.

Barna, George. Born again adults less likely to co-habitat; just as likely to divorce. Barna Research Online. [www.barna.org] (2001).

_____. Surveys show pastors claim congregants are deeply committed to God but congregants deny it! [www.barna.org] (2006).

_____. *American individualism shines through in people's self-image.* Barna Research Online. [www.barna.org] (2007).

Baskin, T.W. and R.D. Enright. Intervention studies on forgiveness: A meta-analysis. *Journal of Counseling and Development, 82* (2004): 79-90.

Bedell, T. M. *The role of religiosity in forgiveness.* Dissertation, The Ohio State University, 2002.

Boice, James M. *Foundations of the Christian faith: A comprehensive & readable theology.* Downers Grove, IL: InterVarsity Press, 1986.

BIBLIOGRAPHY

Bonhoeffer, Dietrich. *The cost of discipleship.* New York, NY: Simon & Schuster, 1959.

Braybrooke, M. Wounds not healed by time. *Theology, 106(832)* (2003): 288-289.

Bridges, J. *Trusting God.* Colorado Springs, CO: NavPress, 1988.

Burnaby, J. *Amor Dei.* London: Hodder & Stoughton, 1938.

Bultmann, R. *Theology of the New Testament.* New York, NY: Charles Scribner's Sons, 1955.

_____. *Existence and faith; shorter writings of Rudolf Bultmann.* New York, NY: The World Publishing Company, 1966.

Cheong, R. *Towards an explicitly theocentric model of forgiveness based on God's two-fold commandment to love.* Dissertation, The Southern Baptist Theological Seminary, 2005.

Cooper, J. *Body, soul, and life everlasting: Biblical anthropology and the monism-dualism debate.* Grand Rapids, MI: Eerdmans, 2000.

Cox, P. *Sacrifice the leader: How to cope when others shift their burdens onto you.* Lake Mary, FL: Creation House, 2008.

Criswell, W.A. *The believer's study Bible.* QuickVerse software, 1999.

Cunningham, B. The will to forgive: A pastoral theological view of forgiving. *The Journal of Pastoral Care, 39(2)* (1985): 141-149.

Day, James. *The tabernacle of the conquering Christ.* Manheim, PA: Sermon delivered at Chiques Church of the Brethren. January 2008.

DeMoss, N. *Choosing forgiveness: Your journey to freedom.* Chicago, IL: Moody Publications, 2006.

Dial, Howard. *The role of suffering in the life of the christian (study guide).* Newburgh, IN: Trinity College and Seminary, 1999.

DiBlasio, F. Decision-based forgiveness treatment in cases of marital infidelity. *Psychotherapy, 37(2)* (2000): 149-158.

Dossey, L. *Healing words: the power of prayer and the practice of medicine.* New York, NY: Harper-Collins Publishers, 1993.

Edmondson, K. *Forgiveness and rumination: their relationship and effects on psychological and physical health.* PhD dissertation at the University of Tennessee, Knoxville, 2004.

Edwards, J. *The nature of virtue.* Ann Arbor, MI: University of Michigan Press, 1960.

_____. *Charity and its fruits.* Carlisle, PA: The Banner of Truth Trust. (Original work published 1852), 2000.

Enright R.D. and the Human Development Study Group. The moral development of forgiveness. In W. Kurtines & J. Gerwirtz (Eds.), *Handbook of moral behavior and development,* Vol. I, pp 123-152.   Hillsdale, NJ: Erlbaum, 1991.

Enright, R.D. and J. North. Introducing forgiveness. In Enright, R. & North, J. (Eds.), *Exploring forgiveness* (pp. 3-8). Madison, WI: The University of Wisconsin Press, 1998.

Enright, R. D. and R.P. Fitzgibbons. *Helping client's forgive: An empirical guide for resolving anger and restoring hope.* Washington, D.C: American Psychological Association, 2000.

Enright, R.D. *Choosing forgiveness.* Washington, DC: American Psychological Association, 2001.

Erickson, M. *Christian theology.* Grand Rapids, MI: Baker Book House, 1985.

Fields, D. *The seed of a nation: rediscovering America.* Scotland, PA: Healing the Land Publications, 2005.

Fosarelli, P. Fearfully wonderfully made: The interconnectedness of body-mind-spirit. *Journal of Religion and Health, 41* Sept (2002): 207-229.

Fountain, D. Bringing faith and medicine together. *Nucleus.* published by Christian Medical Fellowship, Jan (1999): 12-18.

Frank, J.D. Therapeutic components shared by all psychotherapies. In J. Harvey & M. Parks (Eds.), *Psychotherapy Research and Behavior Change,* (pp. 5-37). Washington, D.C: American Psychological Association, 1981.

Freedman, S.R. and R.D. Enright. Forgiveness as an intervention goal with incest survivors. *Journal of Consulting and Clinical Psychology, 64* (1996): 983-992.

Freedman, S.R. and A. Knupp. The impact of forgiveness on adolescent adjustment to parental divorce. *Journal of Divorce and Remarriage, 39* (2003): 135-165.

Bibliography

Friesen, J. W. *Towards a model for forgiveness and reconciliation.* Dissertation, Trinity College and Theological Seminary, Newburgh IN, 1998.

Friesen, J., E.J. Wilder, A. Bierling, R. Koepcke, and M. Poole. *The life model: living from the heart Jesus gave you.* Pasadena, CA: Sheperd's House, Inc., 2004.

Frost, J. *Experiencing father's embrace: Teacher's manual.* Conway, SC: Shiloh Place Ministries, 2005.

Grudem, Wayne. *Systematic theology: An introduction to biblical doctrine.* Grand Rapids, MI: Inter-Varsity Press and Zondervan, 1994.

Hallowell, E. *Dare to forgive: the power of letting go and moving on.* Deerfield Beach, FL: Health Communications, Inc., 2004.

Hansen, T. *When I relax I feel guilty.* Elgin, IL: D.C. Cook Publishers, 1979.

Hargrave, T. *Families and forgiveness: Healing wounds in the inter generational family.* New York, NY: Brunner/Mazel Publishers, 994.

_____. The work of forgiveness: Miles to go before we sleep. *Marriage and Family: A Christian Journal,* 2(3) (1999): 315-323.

Hart, K.E. and D.A. Shapiro. *Secular and spiritual forgiveness interventions for recovering alcoholics harboring grudges.* Paper presented at the annual convention of the American Psychological Association, Chicago, IL. (August 2002).

Hawley, D.R. Assessing change with preventative interventions: The reliable change index. *Family Relations: Journal of Applied Family and Child Studies, 44* (1995): 278-284.

Hebl, J. H. and R.D. Enright. Forgiveness as psychotherapeutic goal with elderly females. *Psychotherapy, 30* (1993): 658 - 667.

Hersh, E. *Christ-centered forgiveness in mental health treatment and relational conflict resolution.* Dissertation, Trinity College and Theological Seminary, Newburgh IN, 2010.

Hersh, E. and R. Hughes. The role of suffering and disability: evidence from Scripture. Journal of Religion, Disability and Health, 93 (2005): 85-94.

Hoekema, A. *Created in God's image.* Grand Rapids, MI: Eerdmans Publishing, 1986.

Hodge, C. *Systematic theology* (Vol. 2). Grand Rapids, MI: Eerdmans Publishing, 1997.

Holmgren, M. Forgiveness and the intrinsic value of persons. *American Philippiansosophical Quarterly, 30* 4 (1993): 341 – 352.

Hong, E. *Forgiveness is a work as well as a grace.* Minneapolis, MN: Augsburg Publishing House, 1984.

Jeffress, R. *When forgiveness doesn't make sense.* Colorado Springs, CO: Waterbrook Press, 2000.

Jersak, B. *Can you hear me? Tuning in to the God who speaks.* Abbotsford, BC: Fresh Wind Press, 2008.

Jones, G. *Embodying forgiveness: A theological analysis.* Grand Rapids, MI: Eerdmans, 1995.

Kendall, R. *Total forgiveness.* Lake Mary, FL: Charisma House, 2007.

Kierkegaard, S. *Works of love* (David Swenson, Trans.). Princeton, NJ: Princeton University Press. (Original work published 1847), 1946.

_____. *The sickness unto death: A Christian psychological exposition for edification and awakening* (Alastair Hannay, Trans.). New York, NY: Penguin Group. (Original work published 1849), 989.

_____. *Works of love* (Howard V. and Edna H. Hong, Trans.). Princeton, NJ: Princeton University Press. (Original work published 1847), 1995.

Kohout, F.J., L.F. Berkman, D.A. Evans, and J. Cornoni-Huntley. Two shorter forms of the CES-D depression symptoms index. *Journal of Aging and Health, 5* (1993): 179-193.

Kraybill, D., S. Nolt, and D. Weaver-Zercher. *Amish grace: how forgiveness transcended tragedy.* San Francisco, CA: Jossey-Bass Inc., 2007.

Kurath, E. *I will give you rest.* Post Falls, ID: DivinelyDesigned.com, 2003.

Kylstra, C. *Restoring the Foundations: An integrated approach to healing ministry.* Santa Rosa Beach, FL: Proclaiming His Word Publications, 2003.

Lane, T. and P. Tripp. Order from chaos: when a bad marriage gets worse. *Journal of Biblical Counseling, 2* (2006): 21-29.

Liu, Felix. *The relationship between Christian wholistic healing in biblical study and pastoral ministry.* Dissertation, Fuller Theological Seminary, 1999.

Lloyd-Jones, D.M. Spiritual depression: its causes and cures. In a devotional *Mind, heart and will*. Grand Rapids, MI: William B. Eerdmans, 1965.

Luskin, F. *Forgive for good.* New York, NY: Harper Collins Publishers, 2002.

MacArthur, J. *The freedom and power of forgiveness.* Wheaton, IL: Crossway Books, 1998.

Mathias, A. *Biblical foundations of freedom: destroying satan's lies with god's truth.* Anchorage, AK: Wellspring Publishing, 2002.

McCullough, M., K. Pargament and C. Thoresen. The psychology of forgiveness: History, conceptual issues, and overview (2000). In M. McCullough, K. Pargament, & C. Thorensen (Eds.), *Forgiveness: Theory, research, and practice,* 1-14. New York, NY: Guilford Press.

McCullough, M. E. and E.L. Worthington, Jr. Promoting forgiveness: A comparison of two brief psycho-educational interventions with a waiting list control. *Counseling and Values, 40* (1995): 55-68.

McCullough, M. E., E.J. Worthington, Jr., and K.C. Rachal. Interpersonal forgiving in close relationships. *Journal of Personality and Social Psychology, 73* (1997). 321 - 336.

McDowell, J. *Beyond belief to convictions.* Tyndale House, 2002.

McMinn, M. and K. Meeks. *Psychology, theology, and spirituality in Christian counseling* (Forgiveness: pp. 203-236). Wheaton, IL: Tyndale House Publishers, Inc., 1996.

Meyer, Julia Erin. *Thesis: Comparing a forgiveness intervention and a psychotherapy condition: The influence of common curative factors on forgiveness and mental health.* Iowa State University, 2006.

Miller W. *Forgiveness: the power and the puzzles.* Warsaw, IN: Clear Brook Publishers, 1994.

Morris, L. *Testaments of love.* Grand Rapids, MI: William B. Eerdmans, 1981.

Murphy, J. Forgiveness, reconciliation, and responding to evil. *Fordham Urban Law Journal,* 27 (5), (2000):1353-1366.

Murphy, J. and J. Hampton. *Forgiveness and mercy.* New York, NY: Cambridge University Press, 1988.

Newheiser, J. Why do kids turn out the way they do?. *Journal of Biblical Counseling,* 3 (2005): *21*-27.

North, J. The "ideal" of forgiveness: A Philippiansosopher's explanation. In R. D. Enright & J. North (Eds.), *Exploring Forgiveness.* Madison, Wisconsin: The University of Wisconsin Press. (1998): 15-34.

Omunga, B. *An overview of forgiveness: a study on the approach to finding true and lasting forgiveness.* Dissertation, Trinity College and Theological Seminary, Newburgh IN, 2005.

Perkins, S. and C. Rice. *More than equals: racial healing for the sake of the gospel.* Downers Grove, IL: Intervarsity Press, 2000.

Pargament, K. and M. Rye. Forgiveness as a method of religious coping. In E. Worthington (Ed.), *Dimensions of forgiveness: Psychological research & theological perspectives.* Philadelphia, PA: Templeton Foundation Press (1998): 59-78.

Piper, J. *Love your enemies.* New York, NY: Cambridge University Press, 1979.

_____. A *generation passionate for God.* Sermon preached at OneDay, Sherman, TX, 2003.

Powlison, D. *Seeing with new eyes: Counseling and the human condition through the lens of Scripture.* Philippianslipsburg, NJ: P & R Publishing, 2003.

_____. Idols of the heart: and 'Vanity Fair'. *Journal of Biblical Counseling, 2* (1995): 35-50.

Prest, L.A. and J.F. Keller. Spirituality and family therapy: Spiritual beliefs, myths, and metaphors. *Journal of Marriage Therapy,* 19, (1993): 137-148.

Richards, J. *Unlocking our inheritance.* Anabaptist Reconciliation Planning Committee, Lancaster, PA, 2005.

Ripley, J. S. and E.L. Worthington, Jr. Comparison of hope-focused communication and empathy-based forgiveness group interventions to promote marital enrichment. *Journal of Counseling and Development,* 50 (2002): 452-463.

Ruth, J. *Forgiveness: a legacy of the West Nickel Mines Amish School* Scottsdale, PA: Herald Press, 2007.

Rye, M. S. and K.I. Pargament. Forgiveness and romantic relationships in college: Can it heal the wounded heart? *Journal of Clinical Psychology, 54* (2002): 419-441.

Bibliography

Sande K. *Peacemaking for Families: A biblical guide to managing conflict in your home.* Wheaton, IL: Tyndale House Publishers, Inc., 2002.

_____. *The peacemaker: a biblical guide to resolving personal conflict.* Grand Rapids, MI: Baker Books, 2004.

Sandford, John & Paula. *Transformation of the Inner Man.* Tulsa, OK: Victory House, Inc., 1982.

Sandford, J. & P. and l. Bowman. *Choosing Forgiveness.* Arlington, TX: Clear Stream Publishing, 1999.

Scazzero, Peter. *Emotionally Healthy Spirituality: Unleash a Revolution in Your Life in Christ.* Nashville, TN: Thomas Nelson Publishing, 2006.

Seamands, Stephen. *Wounds that Heal: Bringing Our Hurts to the Cross.* Downers Grove, IL: InterVarsity Press, 2003.

Selye, H. and C. Fortier. Adaptive Reaction to Stress. *Psychosomatic Medicine,* 12 (1950):149-157.

Shogren, G. Recovering God in the age of therapy. *Journal of Biblical Counseling,* 1 (1993):14-19.

Shore, M. Forgiveness in Film: Finding Truth and Reconciliation. *Word and World,* Winter(2007): 60-68.

Shults, F. and S. Sandage. *The faces of forgiveness: searching for wholeness and salvation.* Grand Rapids, MI: Baker Academic, 2003.

Smedes, L. *Forgive and forget: Healing the hurts we don't deserve.* San Francisco, CA: Harper & Row Publishers, 1984.

Smedes, L. *The art of forgiving.* Nashville, TN: Moorings, 1996.

Smith, E. *Healing life's deepest hurts: Let the light of Christ dispel the darkness in your soul.* Ventura, CA: Regal Books, 2002.

Storti, C. *Figuring foreigners out: a practical guide.* Boston, MA: Intercultural Press, 1999.

Stortz, M. The practice of forgiveness: disciples as forgiven forgivers. *Word & World,* 27 Winter (2007): 14-22.

Van Bragt, T. *Martyrs mirror: the story of fifteen centuries of christian martyrdom from the time of christ to A.D. 1660.* Scottsdale, PA: Herald Press, 1968.

Wade, N.G. Understanding reach: A component analysis of a group intervention to promote forgiveness. *Dissertation Abstracts International: Section B: The Sciences and Engineering, 63* (2002): 2611.

Wade, N.G. and E.L. Worthington, Jr. Overcoming interpersonal offenses: Is forgiveness the only way to deal with unforgiveness? *Journal of Counseling and Development, 81* (2003): 343-353.

_____. In search of a common core: A content analysis of interventions to promote forgiveness. *Psychotherapy: Theory, Research, Practice, Training, 42* (2005): 160-177.

Wade, N.G., E.L. Worthington, Jr., and J.E. Meyer. But do they work? A meta-analysis of group interventions to promote forgiveness. In E.L. Worthington, Jr. (Ed.), *Handbook of Forgiveness*. New York: Brunner-Routledge. (2005): 423-440.

Wampold, B.E., G.W. Mondin, M. Moody, F. Stich, K. Benson, and H. Ahn. A meta-analysis of outcome studies comparing bona fide psychotherapies empirically. *Psychological Bulletin, 122* (1997): *203-215.*

Wampold, B.E. *The Great Psychotherapy Debate: Models, Methods, and Findings.* Mahwah, NJ: Lawrence Erlbaum Associates, Publishers, 2001.

Weaver, A.J., H.G. Koenig, and D.B. Larson. Marriage and family therapists and the clergy: A need for clinical collaboration, training, and research. *Journal of Marital and Family Therapy*, 23, (1997): 13-25.

Witmer, D., *Inspirit vevolution: The art of transformational encouragements.* Xulon Press, 2006.

Witvliet, C. Forgiveness and health: review and reflections on a Matt of faith, feelings and physiology. *Journal of Psychology and Theology*, 29 3, (2001): 212-224.

Worthington, E.L., Jr. (Ed.). *Dimensions of forgiveness: Psychological research & theological perspectives.* Philippiansadelphia: Templeton Foundation Press, 1998.

_____ *Handbook of Forgiveness.* New York: Brunner-Routledge. Yalom, ID. *Theory and Practice of Group Psychotherapy.* New York: Basic Books, Inc., 2005.

Worthington, E.L. Jr. The pyramid model of forgiveness: Some interdisciplinary speculations about unforgiveness and the promotion of forgiveness. In E.L. Worthington, Jr. (Ed.), *Dimensions of forgiveness: Psychological research and*

Bibliography

theoretical perspectives. Philippiansadelphia: Templeton Foundation Press. (1998): 107-137.

————. *Five steps to forgiveness: The art and science of forgiving*. New York: Crown House Publishing, 2001.

————. *Forgiveness and Reconciliation*. Downers Grove, IL: InterVarsity Press, 2004.

Worthington, E.L., Jr., S.J. Sandage, and J.W. Berry. Group interventions to promote forgiveness: What researchers and clinicians ought to know. In M. E. McCullough, K. I. Pargament, & C. Thoresen (Eds.), *Forgiveness: Theory, research, and practice*. New York: Guilford Press. (2000): 228-253.

Worthington, E.L. Jr., T.A. Kurusu, W. Collins, J.W. Berry, J.S. Ripley, and S.B. Baier. Forgiving usually takes time: A lesson learned by studying interventions to promote forgiveness. *Journal of Psychology and Theology, 28* (2000): 3-20.

Wright, H. *A more excellent way: be in health*. Thomaston, GA: Pleasant Valley Publications, 2005.

Yancey, P. *Disappointment with God*. Grand Rapids, MI: Zondervan, 1988.

Visit the Author

H-E-A-R-T for Success Training

H-eart E-valuation a-nd R-econciliation for T-ransformation

Come learn and practice how to use this book as a tool to help people:

- grow spiritually
- deal with offenses
- understand and practice inner person change
- resolve conflicts

Author Ed Hersh and host at Blue Rock BnB Healing Ministry invites guests to join him in exploring how to use the book Escaping the Pain of Offense: Empowered to Forgive from the Heart, as a tool for ministry.

Enjoy a comfortable overnight stay at the BnB and join Ed in several sessions of discussion and prayer with the book as the guide. This interaction with the author can especially help a group leader using this book as a discussion guide in a small group.

Call or email for details:
Phone: 717.872.7440
Email: edward.hersh@verizon.net
WWW: http://healing.bluerockbnb.com